T0328662

Cambridge Elements ≡

Elements in International Relations
edited by
Jon C. W. Pevehouse
University of Wisconsin–Madison
Tanja A. Börzel
Freie Universität Berlin
Edward D. Mansfield
University of Pennsylvania

Associate Editors
Sarah Kreps
Cornell University
Anna Leander
Graduate Institute Geneva

DOMESTIC INTERESTS, DEMOCRACY, AND FOREIGN POLICY CHANGE

Brett Ashley Leeds
Rice University, Houston
Michaela Mattes
University of California, Berkeley

CAMBRIDGE
UNIVERSITY PRESS

CAMBRIDGE
UNIVERSITY PRESS

University Printing House, Cambridge CB2 8BS, United Kingdom

One Liberty Plaza, 20th Floor, New York, NY 10006, USA

477 Williamstown Road, Port Melbourne, VIC 3207, Australia

314–321, 3rd Floor, Plot 3, Splendor Forum, Jasola District Centre,
New Delhi – 110025, India

103 Penang Road, #05–06/07, Visioncrest Commercial, Singapore 238467

Cambridge University Press is part of the University of Cambridge.

It furthers the University's mission by disseminating knowledge in the pursuit of
education, learning, and research at the highest international levels of excellence.

www.cambridge.org
Information on this title: www.cambridge.org/9781009016957
DOI: 10.1017/9781009037938

© Brett Ashley Leeds and Michaela Mattes 2022

First published 2022

A catalogue record for this publication is available from the British Library.

ISBN 978-1-009-01695-7 Paperback
ISSN 2515-706X (online)
ISSN 2515-7302 (print)

Domestic Interests, Democracy, and Foreign Policy Change

Elements in International Relations

DOI: 10.1017/9781009037938
First published online: February 2022

Brett Ashley Leeds
Rice University, Houston

Michaela Mattes
University of California, Berkeley

Author for correspondence: Brett Ashley Leeds, leeds@rice.edu

Abstract: When new leaders come to power who represent different societal interests and preferences than their predecessors, they may pursue new foreign policies. At the same time, in democracies, leadership selection processes and policymaking rules blunt leaders' incentives and opportunities for change. Democracies thus tend to pursue more consistent foreign policies than nondemocracies even when new leaders with different supporting coalitions assume office. Statistical analyses of three distinct foreign policy areas – alliances, UNGA voting, and sanctions – provide support for our argument. In a fourth area – trade – we find that both democracies and nondemocracies are more likely to experience foreign policy change when a new leader with a different supporting coalition comes to power. We conclude that foreign policy responds to domestic political interests, and that, even as the interests supporting leaders change, democracies' foreign policies are no less stable than those of nondemocracies and often exhibit greater consistency in foreign policy.

Keywords: foreign policy, democracy, leadership change, domestic politics and international relations, international relations

ISBNs: 9781009016957 (PB), 9781009037938 (OC)
ISSNs: 2515-706X (online), 2515-7302 (print)

Contents

1 Introduction

In recent years, the world has seen several high-profile reversals of countries' foreign policies. Most prominently, President Trump broke from his predecessor's policies in a variety of domains. He ended US participation in important agreements and institutions, some of which were long-standing, such as the Open Skies Agreement and the World Health Organization (WHO), and some of which were negotiated by the preceding administration, such as the Paris Climate Accord and the Iran Nuclear Deal. The Trump administration expressed less support for multilateral cooperation, took a warmer approach to Russia, and took a more confrontational approach to China and to immigration than the Obama administration. Since taking office, President Biden, in turn, has rolled back several of President Trump's foreign policy decisions. Within days of taking office, the Biden administration announced that the United States would rejoin the Paris Climate Accord and withdraw its notification to leave the WHO. There are also other recent cases of notable foreign policy changes. For example, the Gambia's new leader, Adama Barrow, quickly overturned his predecessor's decision to leave the International Criminal Court; Ethiopia's Abiy Ahmed sought reconciliation with long-term enemy Eritrea; the new President of the Democratic Republic of Congo, Félix Tshisekedi, announced an initiative to rekindle diplomatic relations with the West; and the Philippines's President Duterte declared his desire to "separate" from the United States and seek closer ties with China.

Yet in other cases, leaders continued the foreign policies of their predecessors, even when the policies were initially controversial. For example, despite his party's vigorous opposition to Willy Brandt's *Ostpolitik*, Chancellor Kohl announced that West Germany would stand by the ratified treaties. Similarly, upon succeeding US President Carter, Reagan accepted the Panama Canal Treaties that he and other Republicans had heavily criticized previously. In 2009, Yukio Hatoyama of Japan's Democratic Party (DPJ), despite campaigning on promises for a changed relationship with the USA, ultimately made a deal with the United States to retain the controversial US base at Okinawa, continuing Liberal Democratic Party (LDP) policies.

Consistency in foreign policy, even with leadership turnover, is valuable for a number of reasons. Achieving the benefits of international cooperation often requires countries to make credible long-term commitments; the transaction costs involved in policy coordination and specialization are most worthwhile when the stream of benefits will be lasting. Compellence requires targets to believe that complying is better than waiting for a new leader who will abandon the policy, and deterrence depends on potential challengers expecting new governments to follow through on old commitments. Thus, understanding when foreign policy might change and when it will remain consistent, even in the face of leadership change, is important to understanding a variety of international outcomes.

In this Element, we identify the conditions under which new leaders are most likely to deviate from, or stick to, the course charted by their predecessors in foreign policy. Foreign policy includes a wide range of government actions that affect interactions with countries and organizations outside the state's borders. Foreign policy change can occur when the goals of foreign policy change, but also when the means to pursue these goals change. For example, foreign policy change could involve a movement from a strategy of autarky to one of engagement, a movement from alignment with one bloc to another bloc, joining or withdrawing from multinational organizations, or making or rescinding territorial claims. We examine a range of foreign policies, including those focused on security (alliances) and economics (trade), as well as policies that may touch on both, such as economic sanctions and voting in the United Nations General Assembly.

While some foreign policy change is undoubtedly driven by changes in the international environment, we argue that domestic political dynamics play an important role in foreign policy continuity and change. Within a country, there are different societal groups with distinct interests and preferences, and leaders depend on the support of some subset of these groups in order to hold office (Bueno de Mesquita et al. 2003). As a result, each leader possesses an incentive to pursue policies, including foreign policies, that are in the interest of their *Source of Leader Support* (SOLS). This means that if a new leader comes to office who depends on a different SOLS than their predecessor, we may be especially likely to observe a shift in the country's international positions, alignments, and foreign policy initiatives.

Yet, domestic rules regarding leader selection and rules concerning policy-making affect the probability that a change of SOLS results in a change in policy. In regimes in which new leaders need to maintain the support of a broad spectrum of the populace rather than curry the favor of small powerful groups, it is less likely that new leaders will want to pursue radically different policies than their predecessors (McGillivray and Smith 2008). And in regimes in which policymaking is constrained by a need to cooperate with other powerful domestic actors, significant departures from existing policy should be less feasible, even if an incentive for new policy initiatives exists (Gaubatz 1996; Tsebelis 2002; Lipson 2003). We refer to these two mechanisms as the *selection* and *policymaking* mechanisms, respectively, and we argue that democracies exhibit institutional features that limit foreign policy change according to both mechanisms. We thus expect – recent high-profile instances of significant foreign policy change by democratic leaders notwithstanding – that the foreign policies of democracies are characterized by greater continuity than those of nondemocracies, even when preference shocks occur.

To evaluate our argument, we rely on our newly updated *Change in Source of Leader Support* (CHISOLS) data that distinguish leadership transitions that bring to power leaders who rely on a different SOLS than their predecessors and leadership transitions that exhibit continuity in SOLS (Mattes, Leeds, and Matsumura 2016). The wide spatial-temporal domain (1919–2018 for all countries with a population greater than 500,000) allows us to evaluate the relationship between SOLS change and foreign policy change in four distinct areas: alliances, United Nations General Assembly voting, economic sanctions, and trade. We select these issue areas to include both security and economic issues and to vary the domestic salience of the issue areas, the domestic policymaking rules, and the level of international constraint.

We test two core hypotheses across these four policy arenas: first, that SOLS changes are positively associated with foreign policy change; and second, that this correlation is more pronounced for nondemocracies than for democracies. Our analyses show that leadership changes that coincide with a change in leaders' societal supporting coalitions are associated with foreign policy change across all four issue areas.[1] Furthermore, in three of our issue areas, the evidence suggests that the relationship between SOLS changes and foreign policy change is stronger for nondemocracies than for democracies. There are statistically significant positive correlations between SOLS changes and alliance violation, United Nations General Assembly (UNGA) vote change, and economic sanctions in nondemocracies, but no such systematic relationships exist between SOLS changes and foreign policy change for democracies. Across most models, we further find the estimated substantive effects of SOLS changes to be significantly greater in nondemocracies than in democracies. In the area of trade, by contrast, we find that SOLS changes in both democracies and nondemocracies are associated with changes in foreign policy. While the average change in dyadic imports associated with a SOLS change in a nondemocracy is greater than the corresponding amount of change in a democracy, these two estimates are not consistently statistically different from one another. Our evidence across issue areas suggests that democracies' foreign policies are no less stable,

---

[1] For the sanctions analysis, we only find a statistically significant positive correlation between SOLS changes and foreign policy change when we exclude an outlier case: the United States.

and are typically more stable, than those of nondemocracies, even in the face of changes in whose interests and preferences leaders represent.

The results of our research shed light on several long-standing debates in the field of international relations. First, the relative power of international versus domestic incentives in driving foreign policy is one of the defining fissures in the study of international relations. While we certainly believe that foreign policy responds to changes in the international system and international events, our findings support the view that foreign policy, like domestic policy, is driven in part by the parochial interests of groups with influence on leaders. We agree with Narizny that we should not view domestic politics as merely "a constraint on the pursuit of the 'national interest,'" but instead as "the fundamental determinant of state behavior" (2007:3).

The view that domestic politics exerts an important effect on international relations is reflected in a growing body of scholarly work. Some scholars suggest that leaders with different backgrounds, demographic characteristics, and personality traits will pursue different foreign policies (Saunders 2011, 2017; Colgan 2013; Horowitz, Stam, and Ellis 2015; Yarhi-Milo 2018; Yarhi-Milo, Kertzer, and Renshon 2018; Fuhrmann 2020; Krcmaric, Nelson, and Roberts 2020). Others suggest that domestic institutions determine which kinds of leaders rise to power or push all leaders to adopt similar strategies to survive (Maoz and Russett 1993; Bueno de Mesquita et al. 2003; Chiozza and Goemans 2011; Weeks 2014). We argue that a new unit of analysis, which falls between the leader-level and the level of institutional structure, is relevant to this debate: the Source of Leader Support (SOLS). Leaders with particular policies and characteristics are selected by domestic coalitions and are constrained by the need to maintain support from these actors. Thus, within a single institutional structure, the societal coalitions that leaders rely on affect incentives for foreign policy continuity and change. Focusing on individual leaders may overpredict change, and focusing on changes in domestic institutions may underpredict it.

Our focus on SOLS changes as a time when foreign policy change should be most likely also allows us to address another perennial debate in international relations: whether democracies are prone to fickle foreign policies or whether they make for reliable international partners. Arguments about democracies' volatility date back to Alexis de Tocqueville (1835) and blame frequent leadership turnover and the need for leaders to be responsive to the vagaries of public opinion for the inability of democracies to stay the course (Gartzke and Gleditsch 2004). By contrast, numerous scholars have put forward the view that the policymaking constraints and the rule of law inherent in democratic systems predispose democratic leaders to pursue more stable rather than less stable policies (Gaubatz 1996; Martin 2000; Lipson 2003; Leeds, Mattes, and Vogel 2009). In our project, we shed more light on democratic consistency by looking at the behavior of democracies in the aftermath of changes in leadership that bring to power new leaders with different domestic support groups than their predecessors. These are the exact circumstances that de Tocqueville and others consider to be a key cause of democracies' potentially mercurial policies.

We also contribute to the theoretical literature on democratic consistency by elaborating two distinct mechanisms that induce stability in democracies. First, the *selection* mechanism focuses on how the large size of democratic leaders' SOLS and the need to retain support for democracy shapes their incentives for foreign policy continuity. Second, the policymaking mechanism highlights how the presence of domestic constraining actors can prevent a leader from implementing any desired change. We argue that the greater SOLS of democratic leaders and the presence of constraining actors in democratic polities induce foreign policy stability by shaping both whether leaders *want* to pursue change and whether they are *able* to.

Certainly there may be differences among different types of democracies and among different nondemocratic regime types; both rules for selection and rules for policymaking vary among democracies and nondemocracies as well as across them. We agree with Hyde and Saunders (2020), however, that the broad distinction between democracies and nondemocracies remains useful for understanding international outcomes; there are consistent and robust differences between these broad categories of institutions (see also Svolik 2012). By examining the behavior of democracies and the behavior of nondemocracies across a range of foreign policies that vary in their domestic salience and their domestic policymaking processes, we speak to the utility of these broad categories for distinguishing foreign policy behavior. We find that democracies are better able to combine accountability with foreign policy consistency; it is the accountability of nondemocratic leaders to groups with particular interests combined with few policymaking constraints that makes domestically driven foreign policy change more likely.

Finally, our Element bears on important contemporary issues. The rise of populist leaders in countries such as the United States, Britain, India, Brazil, and the Philippines has caused many to question whether our confidence in democracies for peace and international cooperation is misplaced. Our study suggests that the foreign policy changes embraced by these leaders are somewhat unusual from a historical viewpoint. We find that democracies are quite stable in their foreign policies as compared to nondemocracies, though the area of trade is an exception. Why, then, are we seeing these stunning reversals of foreign policy across a variety of different foreign policy domains? In our conclusion (Section 5), we discuss recent developments in the context of our theory and results. We also address the question of whether we should expect democracies to continue to lead reliable foreign policies into the future.

2 Domestic Sources of Leader Support, Institutions, and Foreign Policy Change

While a country's foreign policy responds to, and is often constrained by, systemic factors such as geography and relative power, foreign policy is also driven by domestic political dynamics (Risse-Kappen 1991; Milner 1997; Moravcsik 1997; Fordham 1998; Solingen 1998; Narizny 2007; Mattiacci Forthcoming). In this section we lay out our argument about the importance of leaders' domestic supporting coalitions in shaping their incentives for foreign policy continuity or change. We argue that foreign policy change should be most likely when a new leader with a different source of societal support than their predecessor comes to office. Whether these leaders will indeed pursue a new foreign policy course, however, also depends on the domestic institutional context. We highlight the importance of two mechanisms that tend to induce stability, one tied to the processes of leader selection and one tied to institutional checks on leaders. Democracies feature both of these mechanisms; as a result, we hypothesize that they conduct more consistent foreign policies, even in the face of preference shocks, than nondemocracies.

2.1 Domestic Drivers of Foreign Policy Change

Within polities, different societal groups with different interests and preferences compete with one another for influence over policymaking. Much of the competition is focused on domestic issues, but societal groups also diverge in their foreign policy preferences. The source of different foreign policy interests and preferences within societies varies from country to country, and may vary across time. Meaningful cleavages often exist, for example, along economic, ethnic, religious, or regional lines. Existing international relations scholarship has shown that individuals affiliated with different factors or sectors of the economy not only prefer different trade and monetary policies (Frieden 1988; Rogowski 1989; Haggard 1990; Simmons 1994; Milner 1997; Bearce 2003), but also different security policies (Snyder 1991; Fordham 1998, 2019; Lobell 2004; Narizny 2007; Solingen 2007). Similarly, we know that in some countries, ethnic, religious, or regional group identities are tied to preferences over international conflict (Davis and Moore 1997) and grand strategy (Trubowitz 1998). Additionally, individual-level characteristics such as gender, education, and race have been shown to bear on particular foreign policy preferences

(Holsti 2006), such as preferences over the use of force (Barnhart et al. 2020) and preferences regarding trade policy (Guisinger 2017).

In some cases, differences in foreign policy interests across societal groups are driven by distributional implications of policies that create economic winners and losers domestically. In other cases, differences in foreign policy preferences derive from nonmaterial or ideological considerations. For example, studies by Haas (2005), Rathbun (2004), and Tingley (2010) suggest ideology plays a role in the preferences of individuals regarding international alignments, peace missions, and foreign aid, and Milner and Tingley (2015) note that ideological divisions affect domestic actors' preferences over the use of coercive versus cooperative foreign policy tools. As Milner and Tingley (2015) conclude, both interests and ideas affect the foreign policy preferences of domestic groups.

Sometimes societal groups are active in demanding that their country pursue particular policies. A case in point is that of diasporas, who often have well-defined views over the appropriate policy toward their country of origin (Smith 2000), as is the case, for example, with Cuban Americans (Haney and Vanderbush 1999). Furthermore, for some countries, such as Cold War West Germany, domestic fortunes are closely tied to international politics, and domestic groups may both be attentive to foreign policy and have preferences about what particular policies are in their best interest, such as whether to seek an alliance with the United States or rapprochement with the Soviet Union (Haftendorn 2006). In recent years, national elections in several countries, such as the Maldives, Sri Lanka, and Malaysia, have also been, at least in part, referendums about the desirability of close ties with China (Moosa and Abi-Habib 2018). Often, however, societal groups do not actively articulate the specific foreign policies they would prefer. In fact, some research, especially in the US context, suggests that the mass public is largely uninformed over foreign policy and does not hold consistent policy positions (Almond 1950; Lippman 1955; Berinsky 2007). These insights have been challenged by others: while voters may know little about day-to-day international politics, newer work has repeatedly shown that they do hold stable and coherent preferences over the types of foreign policies they wish their governments to pursue, and their preferences tend to be based in their core values (Page and Shapiro 1982; Hurwitz and Peffley 1987; Aldrich et al. 2006; Rathbun et al. 2016).

Here we argue that for the interests and preferences of domestic groups to shape foreign policy, it is not necessary for individual members of these groups to be able to articulate which *specific* foreign policies they want their country to pursue. We don't expect citizens to gather information and express a position on every foreign policy action. The politicians that represent them understand how different foreign policies affect the well-being of their backers and what policies are in their supporters' interest. Furthermore, interest groups can play an important role in translating underlying interests and preferences into action-able foreign policy (Milner and Tingley 2015). Interest groups both lobby leaders to implement policies that are desirable from the perspective of their constituents and provide information to societal groups about whether a particular foreign policy conforms to the groups' interests.[2] Our argument depends on the claim that members of the public have consistent foreign policy preferences tied to their interests and ideologies, but it does not depend on members of the public knowing the details of UNGA votes or trade policy. Because leaders understand the impact of foreign policies on their constituents, differences in interests and preferences among domestic groups can shape a country's foreign policy even when individual members of the public do not make specific policy demands.

Within each country there is constant competition about whose interests and preferences get translated into foreign policy. In some countries, specifically in democracies, societal groups with shared interests and preferences band together in political parties that contest elections. In fact, the traditional view of political parties is that they were formed along sociocultural conflict lines (Lipset and Rokkan 1967). While the cleavages that originally motivated party formation may decline in importance over time, parties adapt to reflect new domestic cleavages (Inglehart 1997) or to aggregate voters based on their disparate stances on individual domestic and international issues (Franklin, Mackie, and Valen 1992).[3] Thus, in many countries, competition between societal groups with different interests and preferences takes the shape of party contests. In other countries, specifically in nondemocracies, domestic actors with distinct interests and preferences – such as the military, oligarchs, members of the royal family, and ethnic and regionally based communities – might not create political organizations and rely more on the threat or use of force to wield influence.

---

[2] Public reliance on elite cues is not inconsistent with our argument. What would challenge our argument is if societal cleavages, and thus the existence of different societal groups with different interests and preferences, were entirely manufactured by elites. In that case, SOLS would not have an independent effect on foreign policy. While there is evidence that elites influence public opinion under some conditions (Berinsky 2007; Guisinger and Saunders 2017), it also appears that individuals hold general foreign policy orientations that shape their attitudes independently of elite cues (Kertzer and Zeitzoff 2017). Thus, elite cues can influence public opinion about some policies, but they do not typically reset underlying interests and preferences.

[3] Analysis of positions taken in campaign manifestos provides evidence of significant distinction among political parties in issue stances (Klingemann, Hofferbert, and Budge 1994). Milner and Judkins (2004) show that these partisan differences extend to foreign policy.

In all political systems, leaders require the backing of some subset of the population – what we have termed SOLS – in order to gain power and to remain in office (Bueno de Mesquita et al. 2003). In democracies, a leader's SOLS is composed of those who voted directly for the leader or for the leader's party. In nondemocracies with noncompetitive elections or the absence of elections, a leader's SOLS includes those groups or organizations that have the power, through force or through dictate, to install the leader in office and depose them if they so desire. Powerholders who can appoint leaders in nondemocracies include, for example, the military, party elites, ethnic or regional groups, royal families, oligarchs, and combinations of these actors.

Because in all political regimes leaders are fundamentally accountable to the segments of the population that bring them to power and maintain them in power, they have an incentive to pursue policies in line with their supporters' interests and preferences.[4] This means that if a new leader comes to office who depends on different societal sectors for support than their predecessor, we may observe a shift in the country's international positions, alignments, and foreign policy initiatives. To be sure, foreign policy change may occur at any time during a leader's tenure, since international conditions may change. There can also be some foreign policy change subsequent to a leader transition even when the old and new leaders' SOLS are identical, since leader characteristics and backgrounds may also matter for the conduct of international relations (Saunders 2011, 2017; Colgan 2013; Horowitz et al. 2015; Yarhi-Milo 2018; Yarhi-Milo, Kertzer, and Renshon 2018; Fuhrmann 2020; Krcmaric et al. 2020). However, we expect that leadership changes that coincide with changes in the leaders' SOLS – what we term SOLS changes – should be a particularly powerful driver of foreign policy change.

It is worth taking a moment to distinguish our concept of SOLS from the well-known Bueno de Mesquita et al. (2003) concept of "winning coalition" (W). To some degree, they are synonyms. Both SOLS and W refer to the set of societal actors whose support is necessary for a leader to gain and maintain power. Yet, we emphasize additional characteristics of these groups that Bueno de Mesquita et al. do not consider; as a result, we derive different theoretical expectations. We are interested in the *nature* of the coalition, while Bueno de Mesquita et al. focus on the *size* of W. To the extent that size is what matters, we should expect no change in policy with changes in the

---

[4] We are agnostic as to whether leaders opportunistically pursue policies that reflect their SOLS' preferences because they depend on these groups for office or whether leaders personally share these policy preferences. We do argue, however, that a leader's SOLS exerts significant influence over the policies the leader pursues and that leaders will typically prioritize political survival over personal policy goals.

composition of leaders' coalitions as long as institutional rules that affect the size of W do not change. We agree that the size of the necessary winning coalition matters – it is one of the factors that we believe moderates the relationship between SOLS change and foreign policy change – but we argue that the composition of the SOLS matters also. For example, Bueno de Mesquita et al. deduce that when W is large, leaders have incentives to provide public goods. We do not disagree with this, but we note that different SOLS might have different preferences over which public goods are priori-tized. Internationally, the promotion of peace and security, of infrastructure for global economic exchange, and of human rights and humanitarian aid all share features of public goods but are sometimes in conflict with one another. Consecutive leaders might focus their efforts on different public goods depending on the particular preferences and interests of their supporters. In order to distinguish our focus on the *nature* of the leader's supporting coalition rather than its size, we use the term SOLS.[5]

There is no a priori reason to believe that variance in the nature of SOLS is different across regime types; significant economic, ethnic, religious, and regional cleavages and ideological disagreements among societal groups char-acterize democracies and nondemocracies alike, and political competition exists in all regimes. Yet, there is reason to believe that the *effect* of SOLS changes on the likelihood and extent of foreign policy change differs systemat-ically across different regime types. In Section 2.2 we formulate an argument about how domestic political institutions help moderate the effect of SOLS changes on foreign policy change.

2.2 Domestic Stabilizers of Foreign Policy

We argue that there are two fundamental mechanisms by which domestic institutional rules might inhibit foreign policy change. The first is a *selection mechanism*: leadership selection processes can create incentives for leaders to pursue policies broadly in line with their predecessors' policies, even when some of the leaders' supporters express appetite for change. The second is a *policymaking mechanism*: institutional rules about policymaking can limit a leader's ability to change the country's foreign policy, even when the leader might want to undertake such changes given their supporters' preferences. The selection mechanism might thus be seen as tempering any desire on behalf of a new leader to change policies, while the policymaking mechanism prevents

---

[5] Using a different term is also useful when it comes to operationalizing concepts and collecting data, since scholars may be interested in using data on winning coalition size (W) along with data about the nature of the groups from which a leader derives support (SOLS).

leaders from actually carrying out any policy changes that they might desire.[6] In Sections 2.2.1 and 2.2.2 we expand on these two mechanisms. We argue that the selection and policymaking mechanisms are analytically distinct but that the institutional rules that produce them typically coincide empirically. Both mechanisms feature prominently in democratic systems of governance. As a result, democracies should be less likely to experience significant foreign policy change compared to nondemocracies, even when a new leader who represents different societal interests and preferences enters into office.

2.2.1 How Leader Selection Processes Produce Stability

The first set of institutional rules that moderate the effect of SOLS change on foreign policy change have to do with the rules for how leaders are selected. In majoritarian democratic systems, institutional rules require leaders to obtain approximately 50 percent of the votes, while in parliamentary systems with proportional representation, a lower but still substantial number of votes is necessary. By contrast, in the Soviet Union leaders required the support of only 3–5 percent of the citizenry (Bueno de Mesquita et al. 2003: 53), and, in an oligarchy, powerholders constitute no more than 5 percent of the population (Geddes 2003: 248). In other nondemocracies, the required SOLS size is even smaller: in a military dictatorship, the leader needs the support of only a small number of high-ranking military leaders; and in a personalist regime, leaders may rely primarily on the loyalty of their extended family. Even where multiple powerholders exist – for example, the leader receives support from the military and members of an ethnic group – the leader's SOLS is still composed of a small fraction of the country's population. In sum, the SOLS of democratic leaders are typically larger than those of nondemocratic ones (Bueno de Mesquita et al. 2003).[7]

Holding constant the country's population, the larger a leader's SOLS, the greater the likelihood that the leader's SOLS overlaps with the previous leader's SOLS. For example, in a majoritarian democracy where leaders require 50 percent of the vote, the likelihood that two successive leaders obtain support from some of the same societal groups is high. By contrast, in nondemocracies, where

---

[6] Our policymaking mechanism parallels what has frequently been termed "horizontal accountability," but our selection mechanism is distinct from its counterpart "vertical accountability." We focus on how leader selection processes shape the preferences and interests that consecutive leaders seek to fulfill rather than how domestic institutions shape citizens' ability to punish individual leaders for undesirable policies. Ours is not a domestic audience costs argument, but rather an argument about how different institutions may generate different incentives to stick to existing policies.

[7] Our focus is on the size of the minimally required SOLS. Leaders may sometimes have a surplus of support, but their incentives are driven by what is required to gain and maintain power.

leaders depend on a small subset of actors (possibly significantly less than 1 percent of the population), two consecutive leaders' SOLS are less likely to include the same members.

We should expect that when the SOLS of a new leader overlaps with the predecessor's SOLS, as is often the case in democracies, the new leader's incentives to change policy, including foreign policy, are muted because the new leader needs to appeal to groups who supported the predecessor's policies. Often the overlapping selectors are centrists. Median voter dynamics – originally conceptualized by Black (1948) and Downs (1957) – have been shown to exist in various democratic systems of governance. In the US context, Erikson, MacKuen, and Stimson (2002) find that presidential candidates with centrist policy platforms receive more votes. In a study of twelve Western European countries, Ezrow (2005) shows that voters appear to favor parties that they perceive to be more middle-of-the-road. Looking at twenty-five postwar democracies, Adams and Somer-Topcu (2009) find that parties that move closer to the political center outperform, at the next election, those that do not moderate, and that parties that embrace more radical positions lose votes.

Appealing to the median voter is thus one strategy leaders can use to achieve victory in democratic elections.[8] To the extent that it pays to play to the center, leaders face a stronger electoral incentive to construct policies that satisfy politically moderate voters rather than their base because the former will condition their willingness to support the leader on the leader's policies while the latter are likely to vote for the leader on principle (Schultz 2005). Democratic leaders with different sets of core supporters than their predecessors might choose to change some policies to align them with their bases' preferences, but if the best electoral strategy is to appeal to the center they will restrict the extent and volume of change. By contrast, in nondemocracies, the absence of competitive elections means that there is no centripetal force that could push governments toward a more centrist position. Where election results can be manipulated or voters intimidated, or where no elections occur, the median

---

[8] Leaders might also pursue an alternative turnout-based strategy focused on energizing the base. Such a strategy should be associated with a greater potential for foreign policy change as consecutive leaders will be drawn to policies reflecting their bases' more extreme preferences. Whether a turnout-based strategy is viable depends on the political context, however. Karp, Banducci, and Bowler (2008) show that voter mobilization through party canvassing occurs at higher rates in single-member-district than in proportional representation systems. A turnout-based strategy is also only desirable where voter turnout is low, such as in the United States, and thus mobilizing one's base might make a difference (Holbrook and McClurg 2005); by contrast, voter turnout has traditionally been higher in other Western democracies. We discuss in Section 5 what to expect regarding democratic foreign policy consistency if a turnout-based strategy becomes more common.

voter does not hold sway, and, as a result, successive governments can more easily embrace radically different political programs.

The need to appeal to both core supporters and centrists can also be seen as one example of a more general phenomenon. All else equal, larger SOLS are more likely to be heterogenous. The greater the number of societal groups with distinct interests and preferences that compose the leader's SOLS, the harder it may be to agree on whether and how to depart from the status quo. By contrast, when a leader's SOLS is more homogenous – a characteristic that is more likely with a small SOLS – leaders will face fewer constraints from within their own SOLS to embrace new policies.

SOLS size thus affects SOLS composition, both by increasing the likelihood that the SOLS of successive leaders encompass some of the same groups and by increasing the likelihood that a SOLS is composed of groups with greater diversity in interests and preferences. SOLS composition, in turn, shapes incentives for foreign policy continuity and change. Yet, democracy also has another impact: incentives for leaders to pursue broad-based policies that favor not only their own SOLS but even those outside of their SOLS.

Bueno de Mesquita et al. (2003) developed a formal model that deduces that the size of a leader's winning coalition (W) affects the leader's strategy of distributing governmental funds in the form of either public goods (i.e. policies that benefit everyone in the country) or private goods (i.e. policies that direct resources to particular groups). According to their model, in large W systems, such as democracies, because leaders require the support of a large subset of the population, leaders are better off focusing on policies that contribute to the greater good. By contrast, in nondemocracies, which are typically small W systems, leaders have an incentive to provide private goods to pay off their supporters.

McGillivray and Smith (2008) further argue that incentives to produce public versus private goods affect policy stability. Countries where leaders focus on the provision of public goods (i.e. democracies) should experience greater policy continuity because there is likely to be significant overlap in the broad-based policies that successive leaders will pursue. By contrast, in systems where leaders provide private benefits to their supporters (i.e. many nondemocracies), policy volatility may occur when one leader is replaced with another with a different domestic supporting coalition. In these cases, it is much less likely that there is overlap in the particularistic policies of one leader and the particularistic policies of another.

We agree with Bueno de Mesquita et al. (2003) and McGillivray and Smith (2008) that democratic leaders are more likely to focus on the provision of public goods than nondemocratic leaders are. However, we believe successive

SOLS within democracies may have different preferences in terms of *which* public goods are emphasized. For example, one might be concerned primarily with advancing human rights abroad, while another might care most about maintaining strong infrastructure for global economic exchange, both of which can be considered public goods. The incentive to produce public goods does not in itself mean policy choices will be identical. That being said, there are fewer permutations of portfolios of public goods than there are of portfolios of private goods. Thus, while it does not eliminate the motivation to change policy in response to the interests and preferences of a new SOLS, the incentive to focus on public goods likely results in less foreign policy change than occurs in systems in which the incentive is to provide private goods to a small group of supporters.

Another important distinction between democracies and nondemocracies lies in the reliance on free and fair elections to select leaders. Elections work as selection mechanisms only as long as the losers are willing to respect them. Democratic leaders need to convince the losers of an election that they retain a stake in the system; to persist and function, democracy must be viewed as the most legitimate form of governance by most citizens. If the losers of the last election feel unfairly targeted by the new leader's policies they could become disaffected and democracy might be at risk (Anderson et al. 2005). Because democratic leaders are aware of these dynamics, they have an incentive to treat losers gently and continue at least some of the policies that were favored by the election losers (McDonald and Budge 2005). Thus, democratic leaders need to deliver enough benefits to all citizens for them to provide at least tacit support for the government. By contrast, in nondemocracies, those outside the leader's SOLS can more easily be neglected; there is a greater probability that any challenges can be repressed by the security apparatus controlled by the leader. Leaders have little need to embrace policies that buy the support of outsiders when rule is based more on force than on legitimacy. Thus, in nondemocratic systems, leaders with different SOLS than their predecessors have greater leeway to pursue vastly different policies.

In sum, when institutional rules require that a leader gain and maintain the support of a large number of citizens in order to govern, as is the case in democracies, there is more overlap in the supporters of successive leaders even when their core supporters are different; moderate interests may have disproportionate influence on policy; and coalitions are heterogeneous. All of these features make it less likely that SOLS change results in large policy change. In addition, democratic leaders have incentives to emphasize the provision of public goods and make active efforts to retain the goodwill of those who did not vote for them. This too makes policy continuity comparatively likely.

2.2.2 How Policymaking Processes Produce Stability

Whether new leaders will change foreign policy depends not only on the incentives generated by their SOLS, but also on whether the political system they operate in contains actors who have the ability to limit or block leaders' policy initiatives. While across polities executives enjoy greater freedom to shape foreign policy than domestic policy (Canes-Wrone, Howell, and Lewis 2008), in democracies, executives often have to contend with actors outside of the leader's SOLS who have direct influence on the approval, implementation, and enforcement of foreign policy. We refer to these actors as *constraining actors*. Even in situations where consent by constraining actors is not strictly required for policy change, leaders need to consider the implications of defying them: pursuing a foreign policy that is opposed by these actors might undermine the leader's ability to accomplish other policy goals that do require explicit approval. Constraining actors also often do not need to take visible steps to thwart a leader's policy agenda. Much of their power manifests itself through anticipated reaction (Milner 1997; Martin 2000; Goldgeier and Saunders 2018).

Our approach bears similarity to Tsebelis's (2002) concept of veto players, but we take a broader view of identifying constraining actors within each country. First, Tsebelis's focus is on those actors with the ability to block *legislative* change, while we include actors, such as the bureaucracy, who can obstruct foreign policy change by delay or sabotage. Second, according to Tsebelis, domestic actors are defined by their formal powers and their policy preferences; as a result, who constitutes a veto player varies significantly depending on the issue, even holding the overall institutional setting constant. We focus instead on actors' ability to hinder foreign policy change rather than their will to do so. Because our interest is in foreign policy decisions in several issue areas across a wide array of countries, it is virtually impossible to identify which actors oppose a particular policy change in a particular country at a particular time. While this may lead to an overestimate of the constraints that a leader faces, it seems fair to say that, on average, foreign policy change should be less likely where there are more domestic actors who have the power to impede a leader's policy initiatives than where there are fewer such actors.

Constraining actors exist in all three branches of government.[9] In democracies, legislatures are particularly powerful (Martin 2000). Much of their

---

[9] An additional constraining actor not discussed here are subunits in federal states (Tsebelis 2002; Jensen and McGillivray 2005).

influence stems from their privileged role in law-making. Many country constitutions require parliamentary participation in treaty-making (Verdier and Versteeg 2019), and legislatures also play an important role in bringing domestic legislation into conformity with an international agreement (Milner 1997; Martin 2000). As a result, legislatures wield significant influence over the making and implementation of international commitments. By contrast, when foreign policy change involves the termination of existing commitments, the executive arguably has more legal latitude (Helfer 2019). However, often a leader seeks to break a commitment in order to make a new one (e.g. a different alliance), so the making and breaking of policy are closely tied to one another.

Democratic legislatures also typically control the budget and can deny leaders resources for new foreign policies (Martin 2000). They often have the right to investigate and conduct hearings, which can shape public opinion in opposition to new policy initiatives (Goldgeier and Saunders 2018) and thus raise the costs of policy change. Some democracies require legislative confirmation of high-level executive appointments, putting the legislature in a position to exert influence by holding up appointments. Democratic legislatures thus possess a variety of tools that allow them to constrain a leader whose new foreign policies they disagree with.

While legislatures also exist in many nondemocracies, their role is more sharply circumscribed. They often possess the right to ratify treaties, but leaders can more easily evade these constraints (Verdier and Versteeg 2019). Leaders are less likely to be subject to investigations, and other rights of the legislature are curtailed. Wilson and Woldense (2019) show that, on average, nondemocratic legislatures possess fewer powers – often only consultative in nature – than their democratic counterparts. Furthermore, the composition of legislatures in nondemocracies also limits their independent authority. Svolik (2012, 116) notes that "authoritarian legislatures are ... far from representative of the multitude of interests among their regimes' populations and only rarely seat any genuine political opposition." As evidence for the limited constraining function played by nondemocratic legislatures, Gandhi and Przeworski (2006: 21–22) report that, on average, 96 percent of legislative initiatives of the executive are approved by legislatures in dictatorships, compared to 76 percent in democracies. Furthermore, in a nondemocracy, any legislative act can ultimately be overturned by the leader, and the leader may even dissolve the legislature itself (Gandhi and Przeworski 2006). Scholars of authoritarianism generally agree that formal institutions such as legislatures play a very limited role in policymaking (Gandhi and Przeworski 2006; Gehlbach, Sonin, and Svolik 2016; Geddes,

Wright, and Frantz 2018). In line with these insights, we expect nondemocratic legislatures to be much less able to constrain executives than democratic legislatures.

Constraining actors also exist within the executive branch itself – specifically in the bureaucracy, including the foreign ministry, defense ministry, and the military. There are of course limits on the extent to which bureaucrats can constrain leaders (Krasner 1972; Rosati 1981; Huber and Shipan 2002; Kaarbo, Lantis, and Beasley 2012). Outright defiance is virtually unheard of; yet, there are more subtle ways that civil servants can interfere with policy changes they find undesirable. Given their preeminent role in policy implementation, bureaucrats can employ delay tactics, implement a policy imperfectly, or subvert it through other measures (Saunders 2015; Goldgeier and Saunders 2018).

Bureaucracies are more likely to function as constraining actors in democracies, where they possess greater independence, than in nondemocracies. In democracies, leaders might make political appointments at the level of agency leadership, but the vast majority of civil servants are recruited and promoted based on merit. Partisan balancing of appointees, term limits, and civil service tenure, as well as the legislature's control over agency funding and restructuring, also inhibit a democratic leader's ability to exert control over the bureaucracy (Milner and Tingley 2015). Agencies with a stable professional staff tend to develop their own identity and may be resistant to new foreign policy initiatives that involve departures from agency goals and standard operating procedures. By contrast, in nondemocracies, where the threat of violent overthrow is ever present, leaders prioritize loyalty over professionalism. Dictators ensure the fidelity of the bureaucracy, and especially the military, by stacking their ranks with copartisans, coethnics, or friends and family; by rotating leadership positions regularly; or by purges (Svolik 2012; Sudduth 2017). These measures sharply limit the ability of bureaucrats to constrain the leader. While there is evidence of strong bureaucracies in some nondemocracies such as in the Soviet Union (Bunce and Echols 1978; Hagan 1993), on average bureaucracies are weaker in nondemocratic states, given their lack of independence.

Finally, the judiciary might act as a constraint on a leader's foreign policy agenda. If legislators, bureaucrats, or individual stakeholders believe that a new policy is unlawful, they might alert courts, which can order injunctions to temporarily or permanently block the policy. But courts not only serve as a venue for other constraining actors; they also can intervene by their own initiative. Many countries today require ex ante judicial review of international treaties or permit courts to review agreements after ratification (Verdier and

Versteeg 2019). Courts with such prerogatives – high courts – can hinder a leader from pursuing international agreements that they judge to be in conflict with domestic law.

The ability of courts to constrain leaders depends in large part on whether they can act independently and whether their rulings are heeded (Staton and Moore 2011). Summarizing the comparative politics literature on courts, Helmke and Rosenbluth (2009: 355) conclude that "most accounts reinforce the original intuition that democracy (or its prospect) is usually necessary for judicial independence." In democracies, a single leader does not control appointment of all judges, and appointed judges are loyal to the law of the land rather than the leader personally. Furthermore, courts in democracies have the jurisdiction to decide important questions, and the executive will have to implement court rulings (in the absence of a legislature passing new supportive legislation). These features of democratic judiciaries suggest that courts have significant power to restrict unilateral foreign policy initiatives of leaders if they choose to do so.[10] By contrast, courts in nondemocracies typically lack independence and effectiveness. Autocrats use various tools to limit judicial discretion, such as appointing judges for limited terms, adding new judges to dilute opposition (i.e. court-packing), removing or impeaching judges at will, not granting independent financial resources to courts, severely limiting the courts' jurisdiction, ignoring judicial decisions, or, in the most extreme case, dismissing entire courts. As a result of a lack of independence and limited jurisdiction and influence, the judiciary in nondemocracies is unlikely to constitute a real check on leaders' abilities to pursue whatever foreign policy they or their supporters favor.

While it is clear that each of these constraining actors has more power and independence in democracies than in nondemocracies, some scholars have argued that leaders within democracies find ways to limit their own constraints. Milner and Tingley (2015) point out that some policy instruments are less subject to constraint than others, and thus leaders may avoid constraint through policy substitution. We accept that levels of domestic constraint within a system may vary across instruments; limiting the instruments available for use by leaders who wish to change foreign policy is one way in which policy may be stabilized. Our main focus is not on differences in constraint among instruments within a system, but on differences in constraint across systems; both can exist simultaneously.

---

[10] There is some debate about whether the judiciary shows broad deference to the government in foreign affairs, especially in the United States (King and Meernik 1999; Foakes 2015), but there are high-profile examples from other democracies in which courts have constrained the government's foreign policy regarding, for example, stationing of missiles on home turf and foreign troop deployments, European integration, and ICC withdrawal (Wiegandt 1995; Verdier and Versteeg 2019).

In sum, leaders in democracies must engage with other domestic actors who do not necessarily fall within the leader's SOLS and who thus may have different foreign policy preferences; these actors have the ability to impede policy change. This is less true in nondemocracies, where the independent power of other governmental actors is typically limited and where leaders are more likely to ensure that positions of power are occupied by members of their SOLS. As Magaloni (2008: 715–716) notes: "Dictators cannot be easily restrained by formal institutions such as legislatures, courts, or senates, which will inevitably respond to the interests of those who appoint them."

2.3 Conclusion and Empirical Implications

In both democracies and nondemocracies, the preferences and interests of groups within society differ. When leaders come to power who rely on a different set of societal interests than their predecessors, these leaders may wish to pursue new foreign policies. To be clear, we are not arguing that in every issue area every new SOLS prefers a different policy than every old SOLS. There may be cases in which policies persist over time and across SOLS changes. Our hypotheses are comparative: we argue that periods of SOLS change are more likely to experience foreign policy change, all else equal, than periods that do not involve SOLS changes. We further argue that domestic political rules regarding leader selection and policymaking moderate the probability of change and the extent of change that will occur in the aftermath of a SOLS change. While we expect SOLS change to be associated with foreign policy change, we expect this relationship to be stronger for nondemocracies than for democracies.

We acknowledge that foreign policy also changes in response to international events, changes in other states, and changes in the international system. In some cases, international events may cause citizen preferences toward foreign policy goals and means to change. For example, the collapse of the Soviet Union likely changed foreign policy preferences in a wide range of states. Sometimes international events may be salient enough to influence leader choice also; in these instances, SOLS changes would be endogenous. In Section 3 we acknowledge the inferential challenge posed by endogeneity and discuss our attempts to address threats to inference.

3 Research Design: Changes in Sources of Leader Support and Foreign Policy Change

In order to provide new evidence on the question of when we are likely to observe foreign policy continuity or change, we draw on our original data collection: the CHISOLS project (Mattes et al. 2016). For all countries with a population of more than 500,000, the CHISOLS data distinguish leader transitions between 1919–2018 in which the new leader's SOLS is different than their predecessor's from those leader transitions in which the new and old leader represent fundamentally the same interests and preferences. The large spatial-temporal span of the CHISOLS data allows us to study the relationship between SOLS change and foreign policy change in different domestic institutional and international contexts.

Our empirical analysis focuses on the association between SOLS changes and foreign policy change in democracies and nondemocracies across four different policy arenas: the abrogation of military alliances, UNGA voting, the termination of economic sanctions, and dyadic trade patterns. These four issue areas include both security and economic concerns, and they vary with respect to how strong domestic groups' preferences are over different policy alternatives, how much independent control the chief executive typically has over the policy instrument, and the extent to which policy is codified in international agreements or adopted in conjunction with an international organization.

Trade has historically been seen as a foreign policy issue area with significant domestic distributional consequences, ideological differences, and high salience for concentrated domestic audiences. Economic sanctions share some of these characteristics; they have significant concentrated economic effects and can also reflect ideological considerations, such as preferences for condemning a particular regime or for promoting particular policies internationally. Thus, we believe sanctions policy also generally involves significant and salient domestic political differences. Alliances are an area in which some have argued that variance in domestic political interests should be relatively unimportant in explaining behavior since interests in security should be homogenous within a society (Walt 1987). Others have challenged that view, suggesting that both the overall preference for alliances as a tool of policy and preferences for who a state should ally with are intimately tied to domestic interests (Narizny 2003, 2007). While there may be differences of opinion regarding the heterogeneity of domestic preferences with regard to alliances, it is clear that forming or terminating an alliance is a high-profile event that will garner significant attention domestically. Finally, UNGA voting is often seen as a foreign policy action that is of low salience to domestic groups. While there are exceptions – for instance, some votes on high-profile issues such as apartheid and condemnations of Israeli settlements in the West Bank – the everyday actions of the UNGA are followed less closely by either the public or major interest groups than the other policies we examine. Yet, we argue that domestic groups have interests in the overall alignment and orientation of their country, which is represented by the aggregate voting patterns in the UNGA. In addition, for countries that are less powerful and thus have fewer independent options for foreign policy actions, UNGA voting can take on much greater domestic importance.

Partially because of the different levels of domestic salience, the extent to which a chief executive can pursue policy independently in each of these issue areas also varies (Milner and Tingley 2015). While we argue that constraining actors can limit leaders even on policy issues that the former have little formal power over, their ability to constrain leaders should be greater if they do have formal and direct levers of policy influence. With this in mind, constraining actors such as legislatures and courts are often directly involved in sanctions policy and in trade policy, though there is variation both across countries and across cases as to which decisions leaders can make on their own and which require approval. Because military alliances usually involve formal treaties, the involvement of other domestic political actors in changing alliance policy is also high. By contrast, UNGA voting is an area in which most of the constraining actors we described play little part. While the legislature may have general oversight roles in some states, the casting of UNGA votes is a matter controlled by leaders – though leaders have to work with the bureaucracy to participate effectively in the UN. Within individual states, both democratic and nondemocratic, domestic constraint can vary across issue areas, even if the baseline level is higher in democratic states than nondemocratic states.

The four issue areas also vary in terms of the international constraints imposed on a state's actions. Voting in the UNGA is mostly expressive, and states are under no legal obligation to vote the same way one year as they did in the past. Sanctions policy is also often unconstrained by legal international commitments, but economic sanctions may be instigated by and/or coordinated through international organizations, and in some cases may then be legally binding upon states. In the area of trade, there is variation among states as to whether they have entered binding international commitments such as the GATT/WTO. Military alliances always involve formal obligations under international law.

We believe that policies codified in international agreements and/or adopted in conjunction with obligations to international organizations are, all else equal, less likely to change over time than those that are not. Yet, agreements and organizations are formed purposively and entail costs (Abbott and Snidal 1998; Koremenos, Lipson, and Snidal 2001). Because agreements and organizations are most valuable in precisely the situations in which significant foreign policy change is most feared, it may be in exactly those situations in which domestic politics incentivizes more foreign policy change that international constraints to encourage consistency exist (Mattes 2012). Similarly, as noted earlier, domestic policymaking constraint on the chief executive is more likely in areas of high domestic salience and preference divergence. We recognize that levels of constraint, both internationally and domestically, are not fully independent of the expected effects of SOLS change on policy outcomes.

Despite this, we believe that it is important to examine the association between SOLS changes and foreign policy change, and the extent to which domestic political institutions moderate this relationship, in areas of foreign policy where international constraints are present and where they are largely absent, as well as across areas where chief executives have more and less independent control over policy. Studying the foreign policy behavior of a broad set of countries over a long temporal domain in different issues areas gives us some confidence in the generalizability of the patterns we uncover.

In the following sections we outline our research design. We begin by discussing aspects of our design that are common to all four issue areas: the measurement of our core independent variables, *SOLS Change* and *Continuing Democracy*, and the general framework we employ in our empirical models. We then introduce the dependent variables and model specifications for each of our four foreign policy areas.

3.1 Changes in Sources of Leader Support in Democracies and Nondemocracies

We explain the logic and procedures behind the CHISOLS data collection in Mattes et al. (2016), and our detailed coding rules are available in the CHISOLS Data Users' Manual.[11] Here we highlight some key aspects of our coding rules, as well as some limitations of the data.

We identified leader transitions based on the Archigos dataset v.4.1 (Goemans, Gleditsch, and Chiozza 2009) and then coded whether the new leader had the same or a different SOLS than their predecessor. The rules for coding SOLS changes depend on whether a country is a democracy or not. We identified democracies primarily based on the POLITY IV data; periods in which a state is coded a 6 or higher on the democracy scale are considered democratic (Marshall, Gurr, and Jaggers 2012).

As we argued earlier, in democracies the leader's domestic support base is composed of those who vote for and affiliate with the leader's party. Political parties in democracies aggregate different societal groups with different inter-ests and preferences and position themselves differently on many domestic and international issues (e.g. Klingemann et al. 1994). We should thus expect the

---

[11] The complete CHISOLS data (v.5.0) and associated documentation are available for download at www.chisols.org.

greatest potential for foreign policy change with the election of a new leader who is affiliated with a different party than their predecessor. Within democracies, we code SOLS changes as occurring when the political party of the chief executive changes, with exceptions for interim (caretaker) governments for whom we code no SOLS change. In cases in which leaders do not have party affiliations, we examined secondary sources to determine whether the new leader is the predesignated successor of the prior leader, in which case we do not code a SOLS change. Predesignated successors are leaders appointed by the outgoing leader, vice presidents, or close family members. If the new leader is not a predesignated successor, we evaluated whether the societal groups who voted for two consecutive leaders are similar or different.

Compared to democracies, nondemocracies display more variation in how leaders' domestic support bases are organized. Political parties play an important role in some regimes but not in others, where the leader may instead depend on the explicit or tacit support of the military, of particular ethnic groups or clans, or of powerful families. Thus, in order to code SOLS changes in nondemocracies we need to consider a broader set of potential domestic support bases. Geddes's typology for authoritarian regimes (Geddes 2003; Geddes, Wright, and Frantz 2014) provides a valuable starting point. Geddes et al.'s classification scheme is well suited to our project because their conceptualization of regimes "emphasizes the rules that identify the group from which leaders can come and determine who influences leadership choice and policy" (2014: 314). Geddes et al. identify six different regime types: single-party (or dominant party), military, indirect military, personalist, oligarchy, and monarchy.[12]

Given the overlap between Geddes et al.'s concept of regimes and our concept of source of leader support (SOLS), we code transitions from one autocratic regime type to another as SOLS changes.[13] Within single-party systems and monarchies, we code SOLS changes only when the party or dynasty changes. We also do not code SOLS changes while a single oligarchy rules, or while a single military regime or a single personalist regime is in place. In indirect military regimes, where civilians officially wield power but depend on the tacit support of the military, we use a predesignated successor rule. If the new leader derives support from different civilian groupings but retains the confidence of the military, we code a SOLS change, since a core part of the leader's support base has shifted. Geddes et al.'s (2014) data cover all countries with more than one million inhabitants between 1945–2010. We extended Geddes et al.'s data, using their coding rules, to years between

---

[12] Countries may possess "pure" autocratic regimes (e.g. personalist), or they may be characterized by a combination of different types – so-called "hybrid" regimes (e.g. single-party-military).

[13] We treat transitions from hybrid type to pure type or vice versa as SOLS changes in our analyses.

1919–1945 and 2011–2018 and to countries with a population of between 500,000 and a million.

There are also a number of state-years in our dataset that do not qualify as cases of consolidated democratic or autocratic rule. Some of these are periods of warlordism or foreign occupation during which no single domestic group has clear control of foreign policy. Others are periods of transition, during which an interim government is in power. We do not code SOLS changes during periods of warlordism, foreign occupation, or interim government. Cases that do not fit any of these criteria – that is, they are not democracies, but also are not characterized by any consolidated autocratic regime type, nor warlordism, foreign occupation, or interim government – are coded based on a predesignated successor rule. If a leader is replaced by their predesignated successor, we do not code a SOLS change; otherwise, we do.

In the full CHISOLS dataset covering 1919–2018, 19% of country-years experience leadership transitions, and 9% experience SOLS changes; 44% of leader transitions are coded as SOLS changes. Both leadership transitions and SOLS changes are more common in democracies. Among the 4,689 democratic country-years, there are 1,239 leadership transition years (26%) and 713 SOLS change years (15%), while among the 6,628 nondemocratic country-years, there are 901 leadership transition years (13%) and 334 SOLS change years (5%). SOLS change years constitute 58% of leadership transition years in democracies and 37% in nondemocracies.

CHISOLS coding rules are specifically designed to be applicable to a large number of countries and years. Because we are interested in understanding foreign policy changes that may be quite rare, such as treaty violations and sanctions termination, we need a data set that spans a broad spatial-temporal domain. While CHISOLS fulfills these requirements, its large N character also imposes some constraints on our analysis.

One of the limitations of CHISOLS is that it provides no insight into the direction in which a country's policies are likely to shift. There are several reasons why we do not code the directionality of change. First, we would need to identify one underlying dimension on which we could code directional change, but we doubt that a single dimension, such as the left–right scale, properly captures the complexity of domestic politics in many different countries over a 100-year period. While in some countries the left–right cleavage might constitute the dominant dimension of political conflict, in other countries other cleavages, such as ethnic or regional ones, may matter more, and, to complicate matters further, which cleavage exerts the strongest influence on politics may vary over time within the same country. Second, a single dimension such as the left–right dimension may be useful for predicting the direction of policy change in some areas of foreign policy (e.g. trade) but less so in others (e.g. sanctions termination or alliance violation). This means that the utility of coding change on one underlying dimension for our project is limited. Third, we believe any change, regardless of direction, can result in changes in policy. We generally imagine that conditions favor change when a leftist government is replaced by a rightist government, but a new government that is further left than its left predecessor might also change policies. Fourth, given the large number of countries and years, identifying the nature of the successive leaders' supporting coalitions and exactly how they differ would have been extraordinarily challenging. Instead, we put significant effort into coding the more straightforward question of whether there was a change in the leaders' domestic bases of support. We believe this coding is appropriate given our overall purpose: we want to understand propensities for continuity and change in foreign policy and how those propensities vary with domestic institutions. Directionality, while interesting, is not a core component of our research question.

A second limitation is CHISOLS' coding of preference shocks only at the time a new leader takes office; we do not systematically identify changes in leaders' supporting coalitions during their tenure. Exogenous shocks such as territorial changes might restructure who the leader's supporters are, or leaders might reshape their own domestic supporting coalitions. Our sense is that reshuffling of leaders' domestic support bases during a leader's tenure is far less common and less encompassing than transitions at the time that leaders first take office. When leaders with a different domestic support base than their predecessors assume power, pressures to change the country's policy orientation are particularly strong.

3.2 Overall Framework

While our theory makes causal claims about the relationship between SOLS changes and foreign policy change in different regime types, our research design is not suited to identifying causal effects. We use observational data to look for associations between variables that are commensurate with what would be predicted by our theory. To the extent that these correlations exist across a broad spatial-temporal domain, across distinct issue areas, and across different model specifications, we update positively about our theory, but we cannot "confirm" our theory with this research design. In this section, we discuss some decisions we made in designing all of our empirical analyses to reduce threats to inference.

While there are particularities that result from the different nature of the data and dependent variables in the four issue areas we focus on, we strive to ensure some degree of uniformity across analyses. Several principles guide us. First, we focus on the potential effect of SOLS change right after the new leader takes office. Soon after a new leader takes power, other international actors are less likely to have had the opportunity to adjust their own behavior, and international conditions are less likely to have changed significantly from the predecessor's term; as a result, we are able to derive stronger conclusions about the link between domestic preference shocks and foreign policy change. We also note that the decision to focus on foreign policy change early in a leader's tenure may bias against our ability to find a constraining effect of democratic institutions. According to Bunce (1980: 392), in democracies, it is during the leader's initial honeymoon period "when prior commitments are limited; the chief executive is unusually optimistic, open, and powerful; the new team is consensual and desirous of making a mark; the legislature and the public are uniquely supportive; and when new directions in public policy are therefore more likely." By contrast, Geddes et al. (2018: 36–38, 68–69) argue that early on in their tenure, authoritarian leaders tend to focus on consolidating power and learning about policymaking, making them less adept at implementing new policies.

Second, for each issue area, we code our indicator of democracy not simply based on whether the country is democratic at the time the SOLS change occurs, but also on whether it was democratic in the final period of the outgoing leader's tenure. We refer to this variable as *Continuing Democracy (Contdem)*. The logic of the selection mechanism operates when both current leaders and their predecessors have large SOLS; and when institutions are brand new, policymaking mechanisms may also be under development. As a result, we do not expect democracy to constrain new leaders who might want to deviate from the policies of a nondemocratic predecessor as much as they constrain leaders operating in a continuing democracy.

Third, for each issue area, we first estimate pooled models, in which we assess the correlation between foreign policy change and our two key variables of interest, *SOLS Change* and *Contdem*, across the whole sample. Second, we present interaction models that test whether regime type moderates the empirical association between SOLS changes and foreign policy change. For both the pooled models and the interaction models, we estimate three specifications: 1) a model that includes the key theoretical variables of interest but no controls (Basic); 2) a model that adds control variables that may plausibly influence foreign policy change and SOLS changes (Control 1); and 3) a model that adds to the first set of controls additional variables that are plausible predictors of the dependent variable but should not be systematically related to SOLS change (Control 2).

As noted earlier, using observational data to evaluate a causal argument has limitations. The extent to which we can update positively about our theory based on these empirical tests depends on making efforts to address threats to inference. A particular challenge to our analyses is endogeneity driven by confounders. SOLS changes may be caused by other variables that also influence foreign policy continuity or change. There are three potential confounders that we consistently include in our Control 1 models. First, we always control for regime change – that is, transitions from democracy to nondemocracy, or vice versa. Regime changes are often (although not always) accompanied by SOLS changes, but they also have many other effects on policymaking. We need to be sure that any correlation between SOLS change and foreign policy change is not driven entirely by these broader institutional changes. Regime change is operationalized as a movement from below 6 on the POLITY IV democracy scale to 6 or above, or vice versa (Marshall et al. 2012). Second, we control for the end of the Cold War. This major international change had broad-reaching effects on both the freedom of states to change their domestic politics and on foreign policy behavior. We operationalize the end of the Cold War with a dummy variable for the years 1989–1992 inclusive (months November 1989– March 1992 for the sanctions analysis). Third, we control for whether the state was an ally of the United States or the Soviet Union during the Cold War because we believe these alliance structures both limited the possibility of domestic political change and of foreign policy change. We code this variable 1 for any years between 1945 and 1989 that the state shared a defense pact with the United States or the Soviet Union according to the Alliance Treaty Obligations and Provisions (ATOP) dataset (Leeds et al. 2002). Additional Control 1 variables are described in the research design sections for each dependent variable.

In our UNGA and trade models we further include unit fixed effects – that is, country and directed-dyad fixed effects, respectively – to reduce the threat of confounding. Unit fixed effects control for omitted stable unit-level characteristics that may affect a unit's propensity for SOLS change and foreign policy change; they do not remedy confounding stemming from unmeasured characteristics that vary across time within units.[14] We do not include fixed effects in our alliance and sanctions models, which feature binary dependent variables. Including fixed effects would lead all cases that did not experience variation in

---

[14] The web appendix also presents results for UNGA and trade models that include unit and time fixed effects simultaneously, as well as analyses with no fixed effects.

the outcome (that is, all alliances that were not violated and all sanctions that did not end in capitulation) to be dropped from the data; the remaining sample would be biased, threatening our ability to derive broader conclusions. We note that our specification choices mean that in the UNGA and trade models we focus on within-unit variation, while the alliance and sanctions analyses consider cross-sectional variation as well as cross-temporal variation. This approach takes into account the particular data structures of the four analyses and allows us to consider the relationship between SOLS changes, regime type, and foreign policy change from different angles.

While endogeneity due to confounding is our primary inferential concern, we also attempt to address threats to inference driven by reverse causality. Our argument suggests that leaders pursue policies that their SOLS finds desirable and avoid policies that would lead them to lose support. However, a leader may occasionally miscalculate or find themselves in political peril because international circumstances forced them to embrace unpopular policies. In other words, a leader might change foreign policy, which then leads to their removal from office and SOLS change. There is evidence that leaders who start wars, for example, are at increased risk of removal from office (Bueno de Mesquita and Siverson 1995; Croco 2011). We address this potential concern in two ways. First, and most importantly, we ensure that the temporal ordering of SOLS changes and foreign policy change is such that the SOLS change precedes the foreign policy change. In our alliance and sanctions analysis, we are careful in our coding to make sure coded SOLS changes occur before alliance or sanctions terminations. We lag our independent variables in the trade analysis, and we consider SOLS changes that occur before the UNGA voting sessions in our UNGA analysis. Second, we estimate Control 2 models that include other factors that might lead to foreign policy change, but that generally would not cause SOLS change independent of their effect on foreign policy. Control 2 variables are issue-specific and we discuss them in the research design section for each DV.

Fourth, for each dependent variable we examine the association between foreign policy change and two alternative types of leader changes: leader transitions in which the new leader shares their predecessor's domestic source of societal support and irregular leader transitions in which leaders assume power through unconstitutional means (for example, in a coup or through foreign imposition). Our goal with these robustness checks is twofold. First, we want to determine whether SOLS changes are indeed more meaningful for foreign policy change than non-SOLS-change leader transitions. Second, we want to examine whether our findings regarding SOLS changes are robust if we control for the (ir)regularity of leader transitions. In our view, there is no theoretical reason to believe that irregular transitions per se should cause a leader to redirect the country's foreign policy; rather, we expect that irregular leader transitions are correlated with underlying processes – namely a change in domestic interests with political power – that lead to a break from politics as usual (Mattes et al. 2016).

In the next section, we discuss each dependent variable and detail the specification of the key theoretical variables and additional issue-area-specific control variables.

3.3 Dependent Variables and Model Specifications

3.3.1 Abrogation of Military Alliances

The termination of an existing alliance commitment in violation of its terms is nearly always seen as a high-profile change in a state's foreign policy. It is an action with impact not only on the state's security policy, but potentially also on broader relations (Rai 1972; Mansfield and Bronson 1997; Li and Vashchilko 2010). Alliance abrogation is rare, but when it occurs it is a clear indication of foreign policy change.

Our analysis of alliance termination builds on our earlier published work (Leeds et al. 2009), but uses updated data for both the dependent and key independent variables, allowing us to extend the time frame of the analysis. We also incorporate a slightly different set of control variables that fits the framework of this broader project. Our sample includes members of all bilateral alliances formed between 1919 and 2018 (with the exception of pure nonaggression pacts) (Leeds et al. 2002). We observe alliances during each year from their formation through 2018 or until they terminate; the unit of analysis is the alliance-phase-member-year.[15] Our dependent variable, *Alliance Violation*, is coded 1 if a member violates a key alliance provision and the alliance terminates as a result or if a member voids the alliance before its negotiated expiration date.[16]

We are careful to ensure that we code SOLS changes as potentially affecting alliance termination only when they occur after alliance formation but before termination. If a SOLS change occurs in the last three months of the year, we code the following year as being affected by the SOLS change as well. Thus, we

---

[15] Alliances have multiple phases if their terms are renegotiated during the alliance. Alliance phases that end in renegotiation are considered censored in our analysis.

[16] More information about these coding decisions is available in Leeds et al. (2009) and Leeds and Savun (2007). If the alliance ends for a reason other than abrogation by the member, the case is treated as censored at termination.

assume that SOLS changes have their primary effect within four to fifteen months.

In order to control for potential sources of spurious correlation, we include several variables that might influence both alliance termination and the probability of SOLS change. As discussed earlier, our Control 1 model includes indicators for regime transitions, the end of the Cold War, and Cold War alliance with the United States or Soviet Union. In addition, we control for changes in the state's military capabilities and its threat environment. If a state becomes significantly stronger or weaker, it might pursue a new security policy, and domestic groups might choose to select a more hawkish or dovish leader. If the threats faced by a state decrease, there might be less need for an alliance, and there might be a move to select less hawkish leaders. We code change in power as a dummy variable indicating at least a 10 percent change in the Correlates of War Composite Index of Military Capabilities (CINC) score (Singer 1987) since the last year.[17] For threat, we code a dummy variable for a decrease in threat of 10 percent or more based on a measure originally developed by Leeds and Savun (2007) and updated by Edry, Johnson, and Leeds (2021).

For our Control 2 model, we include several variables related to the nature of the alliance: whether the alliance is asymmetric (i.e., includes a major and a minor power), whether it requires nonmilitary cooperation, whether it takes the form of a treaty that requires ratification, and the level of peacetime military cooperation. All of these variables are derived from ATOP 5.0 (Leeds et al. 2002); the peacetime military cooperation index is explained in Leeds and Anac (2005). We also control for changes in the partner state: whether the partner experienced at least a 10 percent change in power, whether the threat confronting the ally increased by at least 10 percent, and whether there was a SOLS change in the partner.[18] All of these factors may lead an ally to reconsider the value of an alliance. Including these additional control variables gives us more confidence that in a model designed to explain the dependent variable more completely (including by factors outside the state), our explanatory variables remain correlated with the outcome.

3.3.2 United Nations General Assembly Voting

While alliance termination is a rare event and alliances tend to be dominated by stronger states, UNGA voting allows us to see yearly changes in the foreign policy of every state (Vengroff 1976; Moon 1985). UNGA voting covers a wide

---

[17] We thank Andrew Enterline for providing us with access to a prerelease version that extends the time frame through 2016.

[18] Regime transition in the partner is a perfect predictor of failure and was dropped from the model.

range of issues that, when taken together, give a good approximation of the general foreign policy orientation and alignment of a country (Voeten 2000). While we don't argue that domestic constituencies are actively expressing opinions on all individual votes, we believe that the overall pattern of voting reflects leaders' beliefs about the interests and preferences of their SOLS.

Notably, some scholars have argued that UNGA voting may be less informative about foreign policy because some states may "sell" their votes in return for other favors. These scholars argue that UNGA voting is not expressive because it is strategic, at least under some limited conditions (Thacker 1999; Carter and Stone 2015). The willingness to vote strategically, however, is itself a foreign policy decision. Because we view UNGA voting as an act of foreign policy rather than an indicator of underlying "true" preferences, strategic voting is not a challenge to our approach, but rather a key aspect of behavior that we wish to explain.

For our analysis of UNGA voting, we also build on prior work (Mattes, Leeds, and Carroll 2015) and expand the time frame studied by employing newly available data on the dependent and key independent variables. Our analysis includes all countries with a population larger than 500,000 that voted in the UNGA during the period 1946–2018; the unit of analysis is the country-year. Using data on UNGA ideal points from Bailey, Strezhnev, and Voeten (2017), we code the dependent variable as the log of the absolute amount of change in a country's ideal point from t-1 to t.[19] We focus on absolute change because we do not have hypotheses about the directionality of change as a result of SOLS changes, but simply the probability and extent of change.

Because UNGA voting takes place in the fourth quarter of each year, in most cases it is appropriate to attribute a country's voting record in a leader transition year to the leader who assumes power that year. New leaders who take office in December are an exception; these executives are unlikely to have much influence on the country's vote choices that year. For December leader transitions, we thus attribute the country's UNGA voting in the year of leader transition to the predecessor; December leader transitions and SOLS changes are coded as taking effect only in the following year. Years with multiple leader transitions also present a challenge. Here we identify the leader who was in office in November as the relevant executive and code the presence or absence of a SOLS change based on this leader. *Contdem* is coded 1 when the country had a POLITY democracy score of 6 or higher both in t and t-1.

In addition to the variables that we include as first-level control variables for all our analyses, we also control for wealth, economic turmoil, and

---

[19] We use the version released April 29, 2020.

change in military capabilities. Wealthy countries are often democracies (which have more SOLS changes), and Brazys and Panke (2017) find that wealthy countries show less change over time in UN voting on similar resolutions, a finding they attribute both to higher bureaucratic capacity and to a lower susceptibility to vote-buying. Economic turmoil and changes in military power can cause both domestic leadership changes, including SOLS changes, and a reconsideration of foreign policy priorities. *Wealth* is measured as the log of the country's real GDP per capita in 2000 prices and *Economic Turmoil* is a dummy coded 1 if the country experiences a year-to-year drop in real GDP per capita of 5 percent or more (Gleditsch 2002; v.6.0). We operationalize △ *Military Capabilities* as in our alliance analysis. We do not include any additional variables that might influence UNGA voting but not SOLS change. Thus, for UNGA voting, we focus on the analysis of our Basic and Control 1 models.

3.3.3 Termination of Economic Sanctions

Our third dependent variable focuses on economic sanctions, specifically senders' decisions to terminate sanctions without the target conceding the demand. About one-third of economic sanctions end in sender capitulation. As Kaempfer and Lowenberg (2007) point out, senders' sanctions efforts may be driven not only by a desire to coerce another state into changing an objectionable policy, but also by domestic actors' symbolic and/or rent-seeking interests. Because of the stake that different domestic groups have in sanctions and their termination, the assumption of office of a new leader may be a catalyzing event for sanctions termination (McGillivray and Stam 2004; McGillivray and Smith 2008; Krustev and Morgan 2011). Ending a sanctions episode without concessions by the target is clearly a change in foreign policy. Some sanctions terminations are high profile, while others are likely noticed primarily by concentrated interests.

For our analysis of the consistency of senders' sanctions policy, we rely on the *Threat and Imposition of Economic Sanctions* (TIES) data v.4, which covers all bilateral and multilateral sanctions between 1945 and 2005 (Morgan, Bapat, and Krustev 2009).[20] We consider both sanctions that were threatened and those that were imposed.[21] Because sanctions are in place for a relatively short

---

[20] In multilateral sanctions cases, we focus on the primary sender as identified by TIES.

[21] The inclusion of threat-only sanctions is theoretically and empirically appropriate. The economic interests of societal groups in the sender state may be adversely affected by market uncertainty caused by sanctions threats. Inclusion of threats also mitigates some of the concerns regarding the selection bias that comes from considering imposed sanctions, which are likely to feature particularly resolved targets and senders.

period – their median duration is thirteen months – we use the sanctions-month as the unit of analysis. Our dependent variable, *Sender Capitulation*, is a dummy variable coded 1 if the sender terminates the sanctions without concessions by the adversary. Both censored sanctions and instances of target capitulation are coded as 0.

Because new leaders may need to get their bureaucratic apparatus in place to implement a new policy, we allow for a delayed effect of SOLS change. Following Krustev and Morgan (2011), we code *SOLS Change* 1 for the month in which the leader change occurs as well as for the subsequent three months. To minimize concerns regarding reverse causation, we ensure that *SOLS Change* is only coded 1 if the change occurred before the date of sanctions termination (but after the sanctions period started). We also rely on the POLITY *begin date* to code democracy at a monthly level. We code *Contdem* 1 when the country featured a POLITY democracy score of 6 or higher both in the sanctions-month and the preceding month.

As with the other issue areas, our Control 1 model includes indicators for regime change in the sender, for the end of the Cold War, and for whether the sender is a US or USSR ally during the Cold War. We also control for changes in capabilities and economic turmoil, as operationalized above. As with our other analyses, we expect that a shift in power or an economic crisis can cause domestic audiences to reevaluate who they want as their leader and may also lead them to reconsider their country's international policies.

In our Control 2 model, we add several variables that may affect a sender's decision to terminate sanctions. First, we include two measures of sanctions costs to the sender: 1) *Sender-to-target GDP Ratio* divides the sender's GDP by the sum of the sender and target GDPs using GDP data from Gleditsch (2002; v.6) and 2) *Sender Costs* is a dummy variable from the TIES data (Morgan et al. 2009) that indicates whether the sanctions entail major or severe costs to the sender. The costlier the sanctions to the sender, the greater the pressure on the sender to terminate the sanctions, even in the absence of target concessions. Second, we control for SOLS changes and regime transitions in the target. A sender may change their goals in response to a domestic change in the target. Third, we control for a change in the target's year-to-year CINC score of 10 percent or more. Changes in the target's capability might prompt a recalculation of whether the target is too little or too much of a threat to warrant continued sanctions. Fourth, we add an indicator, *High Politics*, of whether the sanctions involve security issues (Bapat and Morgan 2009: 1083). We expect that senders may be less likely to capitulate on issues that directly affect the state's security. Fifth, we control for *Sender Commitment*, a dummy coded 1 if the sender formulates a clear and unambiguous demand and also makes a clear "if–then" statement about what type of punishment the target will have to expect in the absence of compliance (Krustev and Morgan 2011). Sanctions for which the sender formulates precise policy goals and clearly communicates their commitment to follow through should be less likely to terminate prematurely as a result of sender capitulation.

3.3.4 Changes in Dyadic Trade Patterns

Our final analysis examines changes in dyadic trade patterns. While trade patterns are not a direct measure of trade policy, they should reflect government policy decisions (Baier and Bergstrand 2007), and, as a result, we believe they are an appropriate venue for examining our theory. A major advantage of studying trade as a foreign policy outcome for our project is that it is an action that all states engage in every year, similar to UNGA voting.

For our analysis of dyadic trade patterns, we examine states' imports from partner countries for the period 1948–2000. We focus on imports because they are sensitive to pressures from domestic groups, and they can be unilaterally manipulated by governments through a variety of policies, including tariffs and quotas. To create our dependent variable, we use data from Gleditsch (2002) but only include those observations for which import data stems from the IMF Direction of Trade (DOT) data and where we have either "custom and freight included" (c.i.f.) or "freight on board" (f.o.b.) data for both t and t-1. Consistency of sources and measurement units minimizes the possibility that year-to-year volatility is the result of differences in coding rather than real change.[22] The unit of analysis is the directed-dyad-year. To code our dependent variable, change in dyadic import patterns, we follow Mansfield and Reinhardt's (2008) study of trade volatility and use the absolute change, from t-1 to t, in logged imports to A from B measured in constant 2000 US dollars.

We code *SOLS Change* in State A as 1 in each year that the country experiences at least one leader transition that brings to power a new leader with a different domestic supporting coalition; if a SOLS change occurs in the last three months of the year, we code the following year as being affected by the SOLS change as well. *Contdem* is coded 1 for State A if the country is democratic in both the year the SOLS change occurred and the preceding year. Both key independent variables, as well as all of the controls

---

[22] This coding decision leads us to use only 40 percent of directed-dyad-years from Gleditsch (2002). We carried out a robustness check using the full Gleditsch sample minus years in which the data source changed from one year to the next. We report results for this robustness check in Section 4.1.4.

discussed below, are lagged by a year, since it takes time to design and implement new trade policies that then bear on import levels.

Our Control 1 model includes measures for regime change in A, for whether A is a US or USSR ally during the Cold War, for the end of the Cold War, and for economic turmoil in A operationalized as discussed earlier. We also control for whether A experiences domestic conflict and whether there was an armed conflict between A and B. Both of these events can prompt leadership changes and simultaneously influence import patterns.

Our Control 2 model further adds variables that may affect the two countries' trade relations. First, we control for events that might make State B a more or less desirable trade partner: SOLS changes in B, regime transition in B, and domestic conflict in B. Second, under the assumption that countries firmly tied into the Western or Eastern alliance blocs during the Cold War experience limited leeway to redirect their trade, we control for whether B is a US or USSR ally during the Cold War. Third, we include standard predictors of trade levels between states: joint membership in the GATT/WTO, joint membership in Preferential Trade Agreements (PTAs), and A's and B's logged GDP. The conflict variables, joint membership in the GATT/WTO or PTAs, and GDP are sourced from Dür, Baccini, and Elsig (2014).

3.4 Conclusion

By examining the association between SOLS changes and foreign policy change in democracies and nondemocracies across these four different dependent variables, we hope to gain a fuller understanding of the domestic drivers and stabilizers of foreign policy. Each of our dependent variables has both strengths and weaknesses for our analysis: the termination of alliances and sanctions are high-profile policy changes, but as a result are rare events and are nonrandomly distributed across states, whereas trade is common to all states, but an indirect measure of policy, and UNGA voting is common to all states, but some question its importance as a foreign policy action. Considering all four areas also allows us to vary general levels of domestic preference divergence and salience, domestic constraint on the chief executive, and the role of international law and organizations.

4 Results Discussion: Domestic Politics and Foreign Policy Change

As explained in Section 3, we seek to uncover the empirical relationship between changes in sources of leader support, domestic regime type, and policy continuity and change across four different areas of foreign policy. Each area on its own constitutes an important aspect of a country's behavior in the international sphere, and a joint consideration of these areas provides insight into the strength and generalizability of the association between domestic and international change.

We begin with separate discussions of our empirical findings regarding each individual dependent variable. We then consider how SOLS changes compare to two other types of domestic leadership change that may affect foreign policy: leader transitions in which the new leader shares the predecessor's support base and irregular transitions in which the new leader attains office via unconstitutional means. We end this section by discussing our broader conclusions about the role of SOLS change in foreign policy change.

4.1 Empirical Results by Foreign Policy Area

For each dependent variable, we first assess the pooled models that examine the correlation between SOLS change and foreign policy change across the full sample. We then analyze the interaction models that are designed to assess the moderating effect of regime type on the empirical association between SOLS changes and foreign policy change. Across the pooled and interaction analyses, we examine three different model specifications: a Basic model that focuses on our core theoretical variables of interest – *SOLS Change* and *Continuing Democracy (Contdem)* – and the Control 1 and Control 2 models that introduce additional variables to help account for spuriousness and for other factors influencing each foreign policy area. For space reasons, we are unable to display results tables for some of the findings we discuss in this section. These results can all be found in the web appendix.

4.1.1 Abrogation of Military Alliances

Our sample of bilateral alliances between 1919–2018 includes 435 alliance phases, 73 of which end in violation (Leeds et al. 2002). Of 16,506 alliance-phase-member-years, 1,996 (12%) experience a SOLS change and 8,324 (50%) are democratic in both time t and time t-1. Not surprisingly, SOLS changes are more common in continuing democracies than in continuing nondemocracies or transition years: 20% of the former experience SOLS changes compared to 4% of the latter.

Given the binary nature of the dependent variable, we estimate logit models with robust standard errors clustered on the alliance phase, and we include time polynomials to address possible duration dependence (Carter and Signorino 2010). Table 1 displays results for our pooled analysis and Table 2 shows interaction models. Given the difficulties of interpreting logit coefficients,

Table 1 Military alliance termination, pooled models

	Basic	**Control 1**	**Control 2**
SOLS Change (A)	1.318**	1.159*	1.218**
	(0.353)	(0.467)	(0.453)
Continuing Democracy (A)	−2.062**	−2.112**	−1.922**
	(0.373)	(0.445)	(0.421)
Regime Transition (A)		−0.419	0.183
		(0.665)	(0.684)
Δ Military Capabilities (A)		0.918**	0.558*
		(0.264)	(0.282)
Threat Decrease (A)		−0.905	−1.241[+]
		(0.726)	(0.748)
US or USSR Cold War Ally (A)		−0.710[+]	−0.318
		(0.396)	(0.406)
End of Cold War		−0.325	−0.250
		(0.606)	(0.663)
Asymmetric Alliance			0.637*
			(0.276)
Nonmilitary Cooperation			−1.210**
			(0.318)
Treaty			0.0538
			(0.410)
Peacetime Cooperation			0.397*
			(0.169)
Δ Military Capabilities (B)			1.585**
			(0.298)
Threat Increase (B)			0.151
			(0.382)
SOLS Change (B)			−0.607
			(0.536)
Constant	−4.551**	−4.585**	−4.952**
	(0.224)	(0.325)	(0.552)
Observations	16,506	12,883	12,461
Alliance Phases	435	414	397
Log lik.	−438.4	−395.6	−329.0
Time Polynomials	Yes	Yes	Yes
Unit FE	No	No	No

Note: Coefficients with robust SE clustered on the alliance phase in parentheses. $+ \, p < 0.1$, $* \, p < 0.05$, $** \, p < 0.01$.

Table 2 Military alliance termination, interaction models

	Basic	Control 1	Control 2
SOLS Change (A)	1.528**	1.581**	1.669**
	(0.375)	(0.550)	(0.525)
Continuing Democracy (A)	−1.801**	−1.777**	−1.549**
	(0.401)	(0.419)	(0.409)
SOLS Change (A) × Continuing	−0.756	−1.202	−1.263
Democracy (A)	(0.726)	(0.879)	(0.832)
Regime Transition (A)		−0.667	−0.0861
		(0.716)	(0.737)
Δ Military Capabilities (A)		0.930**	0.573*
		(0.266)	(0.284)
Threat Decrease (A)		−0.914	−1.248[+]
		(0.726)	(0.750)
US or USSR Cold War Ally (A)		−0.704[+]	−0.353
		(0.396)	(0.408)
End of Cold War		−0.494	−0.403
		(0.668)	(0.708)
Asymmetric Alliance			0.668*
			(0.282)
Nonmilitary Cooperation			−1.204**
			(0.320)
Treaty			0.107
			(0.408)
Peacetime Cooperation			0.394*
			(0.170)
Δ Military Capabilities (B)			1.575**
			(0.297)
Threat Increase (B)			0.165
			(0.381)
SOLS Change (B)			−0.608
			(0.531)
Constant	−4.580**	−4.616**	−5.046**
	(0.228)	(0.328)	(0.563)
Observations	16,506	12,883	12,461
Alliance Phases	435	414	397
Log lik.	−437.8	−394.6	−327.8
Time Polynomials	Yes	Yes	Yes
Unit FE	No	No	No

Note: Coefficients with robust SE clustered on the alliance phase in parentheses. + p < 0.1, * p < 0.05, ** p < 0.01.

especially in interaction models, much of our discussion focuses on predicted probabilities. Predicted probabilities are calculated using Clarify (King, Tomz, and Wittenberg 2000); where control variables are included, we hold their values at their means or modes. Table 3 displays predicted probabilities and relative risks.

We begin our analysis by examining the relationship between alliance violation and *SOLS Change* and *Contdem* respectively in a pooled model (Table 1). Across all three model specifications (Basic, Control 1, and Control 2), we find evidence that, as expected, SOLS changes are positively and significantly associated with alliance termination. Using our Control 2 model specification, we estimate that alliances are more than 3.5 times more likely to be violated in the aftermath of a SOLS change than when no SOLS change has occurred; the increase in relative risk of alliance abrogation associated with SOLS changes is statistically significant at the 95 percent level. We further find that continuing democracies are significantly less likely to end their alliances in violation of terms. The relative risk of alliance abrogation is more than seven times higher for nondemocracies than for democracies (p<0.05).

Our next step is to consider whether regime type moderates the association between SOLS changes and foreign policy change. For this purpose, we estimate models that interact *SOLS Change* and *Contdem* (Table 2). As before, we find the results to be robust across all three model specifications. To interpret our

Table 3 Predicted probabilities and relative risks of alliance termination

	No SOLS Change	SOLS Change	Relative Risk (*SOLS Change*)
All States	0.03%	0.11%	3.68
	(0.01%–0.07%)	(0.04%–0.21%)	(1.33–7.85)
Democracy	0.04%	0.07%	1.92
	(0.02%–0.09%)	(0.02%–0.19%)	(0.43–5.57)
Nondemocracy	0.19%	1.11%	5.97
	(0.11%–0.31%)	(0.32%–2.74%)	(1.75–14.69)
Relative Risk (*Contdem*)	5.22 (2.21–10.85)	20.87 (3.97–61.16)	

Note: Estimates based on simulations using the Control 2 models, 95% CI in parentheses.

findings, we use the Control 2 model to calculate relative risks. In the case of nondemocracies, the opportunistic abrogation of alliance contracts is almost six times more likely when a new leader with a different supporting coalition than their predecessor assumes office ($p<0.05$). In democracies, there is no statistically significant increase in relative risk of alliance violation in the aftermath of a SOLS change. To test whether the estimated effect of SOLS changes is significantly larger in nondemocracies than in democracies, we compare first differences – the difference in probability of alliance violation when *SOLS Change* is 1 versus 0 – in nondemocracies and in democracies. We find that the difference across regime types in first differences is statistically significant at the 95 percent confidence level.

Next we examine the association between regime type and alliance violation when the country has experienced a recent SOLS change and when it has not. Using the Control 2 model, we calculate that, in the absence of a SOLS change, the relative risk of alliance abrogation is more than five times higher when a country is not a continuing democracy than when it is ($p<0.05$). The difference between continuing democracies and nondemocracies/transitional states is even larger when a SOLS change has occurred: nondemocracies and transitional states are almost twenty-one times more likely to see an abrogation of an existing alliance by a new leader than are continuing democracies ($p<0.05$). We compare the differences in probability of alliance violation associated with a change in regime type when there was a SOLS change and when there was none. The difference in first differences is statistically significant ($p<0.05$). This suggests that democracies may be more stable both when a SOLS change occurs and when it does not, but that the stabilizing effect of democracy may be especially pronounced in the face of domestic preference changes.[23]

With regard to the control variables, in line with our expectations, we find across models that changes in A's and its partner's military capabilities are associated with a significantly greater probability of alliance violation, while provisions for nonmilitary cooperation are significantly negatively correlated with the dependent variable. We also see a weak negative association between alliances with the United States or the Soviet Union during the Cold War and the decision to abrogate an alliance in our Control 1 models, though not in the Control 2 models. Counter to our expectations but consistent with earlier analysis (Leeds et al. 2009), the correlation with alliance termination is statistically significant and positive for greater alliance institutionalization.

---

[23] In a robustness check, we ran models excluding cases of regime transition, thereby limiting the comparison to countries that were democratic at t and t-1 or nondemocratic at t and t-1. Findings across all models are similar to those reported here.

Surprisingly, we also find a positive correlation between asymmetric alliances and alliance termination. In some models there is weak indication that states may be less likely to abandon their alliance commitments when the threat they face declines. Regime transition, the end of the Cold War, the formality of the alliance commitment, increases in threat for the partner, and SOLS changes in the partner do not appear to affect decisions to terminate alliances.

Overall, our results provide support for our theoretical argument. SOLS changes are significantly positively correlated with alliance violation, suggesting that domestic preference change can create incentives to abandon existing security policies. We further find that SOLS changes are systematically correlated with a greater propensity of nondemocracies to violate their alliances, while there is no clear association between SOLS changes and security policy continuity or change in democracies. SOLS changes in democratic states may occasionally prompt a reconsideration of existing alliance ties, but often alliances survive transitions that bring to power new leaders with a different domestic support base. Our results regarding alliance violation are remarkably similar to those presented in our earlier study that used a shorter spatial-temporal domain (Leeds et al. 2009).

4.1.2 Change in UNGA Ideal Points

Our UNGA voting data spans 168 countries between 1946–2018, for a total of 8,714 country-year observations. Our dependent variable is the log of the year-to-year absolute change in a country's ideal point as estimated by Bailey et al. (2017). The mean value of the DV is –2.3 with a standard deviation of 1.2; values in our dataset range from –11.0 to 0.81. Given the continuous nature of the dependent variable, we opt for OLS regression. We include country fixed effects and estimate robust standard errors clustered on the country.

SOLS changes occur in 797 (9%) country-year observations, and 3,679 (42%) country-years are continuing democracies. 470 (13%) democratic country-years and 327 (6%) nondemocratic country-years see a SOLS change. These descriptive statistics reflect the Basic model; for our Control 1 model, the temporal domain is truncated at 2011 due to data availability, leading us to lose 1,134 observations. As explained in Section 3, we estimate only Basic and Control 1 models for this dependent variable.

We begin our analysis with the pooled models in Table 4. In the Basic model, *SOLS Change* is positive but only marginally statistically significant (p=0.08); in the Control 1 model, it is significant at the 95 percent level. In both models, *Contdem* is negative and highly statistically significant. These findings are broadly in line with our theoretical expectations.

Table 4 Change in UNGA ideal points, pooled models

	Basic	Control 1
SOLS Change	0.094[+]	0.135*
	(0.054)	(0.055)
Continuing Democracy	−0.495**	−0.290**
	(0.057)	(0.066)
Regime Transition		−0.088
		(0.117)
US or USSR Cold War Ally		0.274**
		(0.063)
Δ Military Capabilities		0.103*
		(0.049)
Economic Turmoil		−0.071
		(0.052)
Wealth		−0.356**
		(0.055)
End of Cold War		0.028
		(0.060)
Constant	−2.147**	0.662
	(0.025)	(0.459)
Observations	8,714	7,369
Adjusted R^2	0.017	0.036
Country FE	Yes	Yes

Note: Coefficients with robust SE clustered on the country in parentheses.
$+ p < 0.1$, $* p < 0.05$, $** p < 0.01$.

Next we examine interaction models to analyze whether regime type moderates the association between SOLS change and change in UNGA ideal points (Table 5). Both the Basic and the Control 1 models indicate that SOLS changes are associated with greater year-to-year changes in UNGA ideal points in nondemocracies, but not in democracies. The marginal effect of *SOLS Change* is statistically significant in the former (p<0.05), but not in the latter. The coefficient of the interaction term also provides evidence that the size of the effect of *SOLS Change* may be larger for nondemocracies than for democracies. In the Basic model, the interaction term is weakly significant at the 90 percent level, and in the Control 1 model it is significant at the 95 percent level. We also find that the marginal effect of *Contdem* is statistically significant and negative both in SOLS-change years (p<0.01) and non-SOLS-change years (p<0.01). The stabilizing effect of *Contdem* on UNGA voting patterns may be more pronounced when there is a SOLS change than when there isn't: the marginal

Table 5 Change in UNGA ideal points, interaction models

	Basic	**Control 1**
SOLS Change	0.203*	0.279**
	(0.085)	(0.090)
Continuing Democracy	−0.474**	−0.271**
	(0.060)	(0.067)
SOLS Change × Continuing Democracy	−0.189$^+$	−0.242*
	(0.106)	(0.115)
Regime Transition		−0.167
		(0.124)
US or USSR Cold War Ally		0.272**
		(0.063)
Δ Military Capabilities		0.103*
		(0.049)
Economic Turmoil		−0.072
		(0.052)
Wealth		−0.354**
		(0.055)
End of Cold War		0.027
		(0.060)
Constant	−2.156**	0.640
	(0.0257)	(0.457)
Observations	8,714	7,369
Adjusted R^2	0.017	0.037
Country FE	Yes	Yes

Note: Coefficients with robust SE clustered on the country in parentheses. + p < 0.1, * p < 0.05, ** p < 0.01.

effect of *Contdem* is larger when *SOLS Change*=1 than when *SOLS Change*=0, (p<0.1 in the Basic model and p<0.05 in the Control 1 model).[24]

With regard to the control variables, we find that *Wealth* is negative and statistically significant. This supports the argument of Brazys and Panke (2017). Furthermore, as expected, changes in a country's power from year to year are positively associated with vote change. Counter to expectations, however, alliances with the United States or Soviet Union during the Cold War are associated with more vote change, and regime transitions, economic turmoil, and the end of the Cold War are not statistically significant.

---

[24] The results are robust to dropping cases of regime transition. Results are also robust in models that include both unit and year fixed effects and models that include no fixed effects.

As with our analysis of military alliances, we find support for the idea that domestic leadership changes that bring to power new leaders serving different constituencies than their predecessors may prompt foreign policy change. Regime type appears to moderate this relationship: SOLS changes are significantly correlated with changes in UNGA voting patterns in non-democracies, while there is no such systematic association for continuing democracies. Unlike our analysis of military alliances, which focuses on one very specific foreign policy action, UNGA voting covers a wide swath of issues and thus allows us to see whether a country may change its broader foreign policy profile in response to domestic changes in interests. Our analysis suggests that domestic preference changes in combination with the domestic institutional setting in which leaders operate may indeed influence countries' broader positioning in the international arena. Our conclusions here are largely in line with those reported in our previous study of UNGA voting that covered a more limited number of years (Mattes et al. 2015).

4.1.3 Sender Termination of Economic Sanctions

Our analysis of sender decisions to terminate economic sanctions in the absence of target concessions considers 896 sanctions cases between 1945 and 2005 included in the TIES v.4 data (Morgan et al. 2009). Sender capitulation of economic sanctions occurs in 301 cases. Due to the relatively short duration of sanctions episodes, we analyze the sanctions-month. The sample includes 27,608 sanctions-months, of which 890 (3%) experience a SOLS change that month or in the preceding three months; 23,733 (86%) observations are considered continuing democracies. Again, SOLS changes are more common in continuing democracies than in nondemocracies or transitional years: about 4 percent of democratic sanctions-months experience a SOLS change compared to 1 percent of nondemocratic or regime transition sanctions-months.

The proportion of continuing democracies is notably higher in this sample than for our other dependent variables. Sanctions have traditionally been a tool favored by wealthy democracies with significant market power. The main initiator of sanctions is by far the United States: it is identified as the primary sender in 18,326 (66%) observations. To ensure that the US case is not driving our findings, we run our analyses both including and excluding sanctions in which the United States is the primary sender.

We estimate logit models with time polynomials and report standard errors clustered on the sanctions case. Table 6 shows findings from the pooled models

Table 6 Sender termination of economic sanctions, pooled models

	Sample Incl. United States			Sample Excl. United States		
	Basic	**Control 1**	**Control 2**	**Basic**	**Control 1**	**Control 2**
SOLS Change (A)	0.076	0.004	0.191	1.317**	1.304**	1.315**
	(0.333)	(0.350)	(0.362)	(0.398)	(0.449)	(0.450)
Continuing Democracy (A)	−0.534**	−0.491**	−0.013	−0.221	−0.261	0.006
	(0.155)	(0.185)	(0.235)	(0.186)	(0.223)	(0.262)
Δ Military Capabilities (A)		−0.400	−0.440		−0.551	−0.767*
		(0.323)	(0.334)		(0.362)	(0.343)
Economic Turmoil (A)		0.451	0.126		0.306	0.117
		(0.289)	(0.313)		(0.292)	(0.329)
Regime Transition (A)		0.723	0.250		0.196	−0.189
		(0.499)	(0.685)		(0.577)	(0.750)
US or USSR Cold War Ally (A)		−0.399*	−0.095		−0.075	−0.308
		(0.184)	(0.246)		(0.222)	(0.294)
End of Cold War		−0.569[+]	−0.433		−0.607	−0.661
		(0.306)	(0.343)		(0.447)	(0.479)
Δ Military Capabilities (B)			−0.405			0.338
			(0.265)			(0.355)

Table 6 (cont.)

	(1)	(2)	(3)	(4)	(5)	(6)
Regime Transition (B)			0.148			0.860+
			(0.389)			(0.468)
SOLS Change (B)			0.252			0.012
			(0.333)			(0.586)
Sender-to-Target GDP Ratio			−0.703*			−0.655*
			(0.292)			(0.333)
Sender Costs			0.343			0.494
			(0.328)			(0.374)
High Politics			0.454**			0.727**
			(0.147)			(0.268)
Sender Commitment			−0.541**			−0.130
			(0.165)			(0.275)
Constant	−3.163**	−2.784**	−2.676**	−2.822**	−2.640**	−2.718**
	(0.158)	(0.258)	(0.280)	(0.194)	(0.303)	(0.319)
Observations	27,608	26,771	23,258	9,282	8,862	7,714
Sanctions Cases	896	857	740	359	340	299
Log lik.	−1565.0	−1506.1	−1248.4	−647.1	−614.9	−538.6
Time Polynomials	Yes	Yes	Yes	Yes	Yes	Yes
Unit FE	No	No	No	No	No	No

Note: Coefficients with robust SE clustered on the sanctions case in parentheses. + p < 0.1,
* p < 0.05, ** p < 0.01.

and Table 7 displays results from the interaction models. The first three columns in each table focus on the sample that includes the United States, while the latter three columns show results when US cases are dropped. For substantive interpretation, we again rely on predicted probabilities and relative risks (Table 8).

As Table 6 shows, we find important differences across our pooled models depending on whether we include or exclude US cases. In the Basic, Control 1, and Control 2 models, when we include US cases, we find that the coefficient for *SOLS Change* is not statistically significant. While *Contdem* is negatively and significantly associated with the probability of sender capitulation in the Basic and Control 1 models, this finding does not hold in the Control 2 model. When we exclude US cases from our analysis, we consistently find no evidence of a relationship between *Contdem* and the dependent variable. However, *SOLS Change* is positive and significant across all three model specifications. Based on our estimates from the Control 2 model excluding US cases, the probability of sanctions termination is about four times greater when there was a recent SOLS change than when there was not ($p<0.05$).

The patterns we uncover by including or excluding US cases suggest that, compared to other countries, US sanctions policy is quite stable, even when transitions between Democratic and Republican presidents occur. It is possible that the unique US role as hegemon during the period of observation makes it less likely to capitulate, or it is possible that particular features of American politics, such as the strong role of Congress in the imposition of sanctions, create more stability in US sanctions policy.[25] Indeed, the results – especially the finding that *Contdem* is not significantly negatively correlated with sender capitulation when US cases are dropped – raise questions about whether other democracies lead equally stable sanctions policies. We turn to our analysis of the interaction between *SOLS Change* and *Contdem* – shown in Table 7 – to see if it can help us shed more light on this question.

Because interaction terms are not straightforward to interpret in nonlinear models, our discussion focuses on differences in predicted probabilities associated with different case profiles. For space reasons, Table 8 shows only the substantive results for the Control 2 specification on the sample that excludes the United States. In some cases, there are estimated effects that we report in the text that cannot be found in Table 8; these are available in the web appendix.

---

[25] Descriptive statistics suggest that the legislature more frequently plays a role in sanctions in the US compared to other democracies: almost 40 percent of US sanctions-months in our sample involved the legislature, compared to only about 8 percent of sanctions-months involving other continuing democracies.

Table 7 Sender termination of economic sanctions, interaction models

	Sample Incl. United States			Sample Excl. United States		
	Basic	Control 1	Control 2	Basic	Control 1	Control 2
SOLS Change (A)	2.019**	2.281**	2.659**	2.101**	2.557**	2.597**
	(0.539)	(0.630)	(0.647)	(0.592)	(0.648)	(0.603)
Continuing Democracy (A)	−0.446**	−0.423*	0.081	−0.145	−0.175	0.117
	(0.159)	(0.188)	(0.237)	(0.192)	(0.227)	(0.270)
SOLS Change (A) × Continuing Democracy (A)	−2.568**	−2.910**	−3.111**	−1.235	−1.807*	−1.843*
	(0.705)	(0.775)	(0.782)	(0.785)	(0.823)	(0.807)
Δ Military Capabilities (A)		−0.480	−0.577^{+}		−0.680*	−0.927**
		(0.307)	(0.329)		(0.346)	(0.345)
Economic Turmoil (A)		0.393	0.080		0.303	0.095
		(0.305)	(0.327)		(0.302)	(0.340)
Regime Transition (A)		0.489	−0.086		0.097	−0.315
		(0.600)	(0.844)		(0.657)	(0.832)
US or USSR Cold War Ally (A)		−0.413*	−0.088		−0.089	−0.305
		(0.184)	(0.246)		(0.219)	(0.292)
End of Cold War		−0.611*	−0.477		−0.679	−0.767
		(0.300)	(0.337)		(0.427)	(0.483)

	(1)	(2)	(3)	(4)	(5)	(6)
Δ Military Capabilities (B)			−0.427			0.328
			(0.262)			(0.357)
Regime Transition (B)			0.103			0.772+
			(0.367)			(0.455)
SOLS Change (B)			0.244			0.003
			(0.333)			(0.593)
Sender-to-Target GDP Ratio			−0.719*			−0.688*
			(0.293)			(0.337)
Sender Costs			0.355			0.515
			(0.331)			(0.373)
High Politics			0.441**			0.721**
			(0.148)			(0.272)
Sender Commitment			−0.579**			−0.203
			(0.169)			(0.293)
Constant	−3.233**	−2.812**	−2.710**	−2.861**	−2.655**	−2.717**
	(0.164)	(0.262)	(0.287)	(0.199)	(0.304)	(0.324)
Observations	27,608	26,771	23,258	9,282	8,862	7,714
Sanctions Cases	896	857	740	359	340	299
Log lik.	−1558.9	−1498.9	−1240.5	−645.6	−612.0	−535.6
Time Polynomials	Yes	Yes	Yes	Yes	Yes	Yes
Unit FE	No	No	No	No	No	No

Note: Coefficients with robust SE clustered on the sanctions case in parentheses. + p < 0.1,
* p < 0.05, ** p < 0.01.

Table 8 Predicted probabilities and relative risks of sender termination of sanctions

	No SOLS Change	SOLS Change	Relative Risk (*SOLS Change*)
All States	0.53%	2.08%	4.01
	(0.27%–0.90%)	(0.68%–4.55%)	(1.59–8.55)
Democracy	0.56%	1.40%	2.49
	(0.29%–1.03%)	(0.32%–4.25%)	(0.62–7.01)
Nondemocracy	0.50%	7.03%	14.46
	(0.23%–0.91%)	(1.54%–19.63%)	(3.92–36.92)
Relative Risk	0.92	6.86	
(*Contdem*)	(0.50–1.48)	(1.19–24.25)	

Note: Estimates based on simulations using the Control 2 models, excluding US cases, 95% CI in parentheses.

Across our interaction models, irrespective of model specification (Basic, Control 1, and Control 2) or sample (United States included or dropped), we find that *SOLS change* is not significantly correlated at conventional 95 percent confidence levels with sanctions capitulation in continuing democracies. By contrast, irrespective of model specification and sample, we find a statistically significant positive correlation between SOLS changes and the dependent variable for nondemocracies. We estimate that the probability of sanctions capitulation by a nondemocratic sender is around fifteen times higher in the aftermath of a SOLS change than when no SOLS change has occurred ($p<0.05$). To test whether the estimated effect of SOLS changes differs across regime types, we compare the first difference in probability of sender capitulation when SOLS change equals 1 versus 0 in nondemocracies to the equivalent estimate for democracies. The difference across regime types in first differences associated with a change in the value of *SOLS Change* is statistically significant at a 95 percent level of confidence in five of the six models.

While these findings are in line with our theoretical expectations, an important caveat is in order. As discussed at the beginning of this section, there are very few sanctions cases initiated by nondemocracies and thus, not surprisingly, there are very few SOLS changes in nondemocratic senders. *SOLS Change* is coded 1 in thirty-nine nondemocratic sanctions-months, reflecting only fifteen unique SOLS changes. A closer look at our data reveals that the finding on the relationship between SOLS changes and sender capitulation in nondemocracies is driven by one very high-profile case: the 1991 Soviet transition between Gorbachev and Yeltsin. We thus cannot conclude that sanctions efforts of nondemocratic senders are generally sensitive to SOLS changes; the converse, of course, is also true. There simply are not enough cases to derive conclusions about whether SOLS change and sanctions capitulation are correlated or not in nondemocracies.

The sparsity of nondemocratic sanctions cases should also be kept in mind when we examine the relationship between *Contdem* and sanctions capitulation in the presence and absence of SOLS changes. Here, irrespective of specification and sample, we consistently find that nondemocracies are more likely to terminate their sanctions efforts compared to continuing democracies when a new leader with a different SOLS recently assumed office. Based on the Control 2 specification utilizing the sample excluding US cases, we estimate that, when there has recently been a SOLS change, the probability of sanctions capitulation is nearly seven times higher in a nondemocracy than in a democracy ($p<0.05$). By contrast, in the absence of a SOLS change, only two models – the Basic and Control 1 models for the sample that includes US cases – show a significantly higher probability of capitulation of nondemocracies compared to democracies. The remaining four models do not show any indication that continuing democracies lead more stable sanctions policies than nondemocracies when there has not been a SOLS change. The first differences associated with a change in the value of *Contdem* from 0 to 1 in the sample of SOLS-change observations compared to the sample of non-SOLS-change observations is statistically different at the 95 percent level in all but one model (the Basic model excluding US cases). Taken together, these findings suggest that democratic institutions might contribute more to foreign policy stability when the country experiences a preference shock as a result of a SOLS change than in times in which the domestic interests that leaders represent do not change. Of course, we reiterate that these results should be seen as tentative given the few nondemocratic sanctions cases in the data.[26]

With regard to the control variables, we consistently find that the coefficient for *GDP Ratio* is negative and statistically significant, suggesting that a sender who is wealthier relative to the target is less likely to cease sanctions without gaining target concessions. This finding is in line with our theoretical expectations. But we also find, counter to expectations, that senders are more likely to

---

[26] Dropping cases in which *Regtrans*=1 does not substantially affect any of the results reported.

capitulate on security issues than other issues. The coefficient for *High Politics* is positive and statistically significant. While some of the other control variables are significantly correlated with the dependent variable in some of the models, the findings are inconsistent across the samples.

Our sanctions analysis produces less conclusive results than our analyses of military alliances and UNGA voting. The lack of nondemocratic senders means that we cannot reliably assess the relationship between SOLS changes and sanctions capitulation in nondemocracies. We find that, as expected, the correlation is positive and significant, but this finding is driven by one high-profile SOLS change. More data would be necessary to determine whether this case reflects a broader pattern of inconsistency among nondemocratic senders. It will be interesting to reexamine this question as we see nondemocracies such as China and Russia increasingly turn to sanctions as a tool of coercive statecraft.

Our sanctions analysis is also complicated by the fact that one country – the United States – accounts for the lion's share of sanctions cases in our data, though the data also include information on the sanctions efforts of thirty-four other democracies. Across all analyses, including and excluding the United States, we find no indication of a systematic relationship between SOLS changes and sanctions capitulation in democracies. Of course, it is possible that SOLS changes lead to a change in sanctions policy in some democracies at some points in time, but overall the correlation between SOLS changes and foreign policy change is weak and inconsistent for democracies.

4.1.4 Change in Dyadic Import Patterns

Using directed-dyadic import data for 1948–2000 (Gleditsch 2002), we examine the respective relationships of *SOLS Change* and *Contdem* with *Changes in Import Patterns*, measured as the absolute change in logged imports to State A from State B in constant 2000 US dollars from t-1 to t. We estimate OLS regression models including directed-dyad fixed effects and robust standards errors clustered on the directed-dyad. All independent variables are lagged one year.

We report descriptives based on the sample used for our Basic model. This sample includes 401,492 observations. *Changes in Import Patterns* has a mean of 0.9, a standard deviation of 1.8, and ranges between 0 and 16.1. *SOLS Change* is coded 1 in 49,440 (12%) of directed-dyadic years and *Contdem* is coded 1 in 184,980 observations (46%). As before, the incidence of SOLS changes is greater in continuing democracies than in continuing nondemocracies/transition years: 30,909 (17%) of the former experience a SOLS change compared to 18,531 (9%) of the latter.

Table 9 paints a consistent picture across our pooled models. In the Basic, Control 1, and Control 2 models, *SOLS Change* is positively and significantly correlated with greater changes in year-to-year volume of imports by country A from country B; *Contdem* is negatively and significantly correlated with the dependent variable. These findings are in line with our theoretical expectations.

We now turn to the interaction models displayed in Table 10. In the Basic, Control 1, and Control 2 models, we find that the marginal effect of *SOLS Change* is positive and highly statistically significant in nondemocracies ($p < 0.01$), as well as in democracies ($p < 0.05$). Across specifications, the marginal effect of *SOLS Change* in nondemocracies is at least twice the size of the marginal effect of *SOLS Change* in democracies. In the Basic and Control 1 models, the two marginal effects are statistically different from one another ($p < 0.05$) but there is no statistically significant difference in their sizes in the Control 2 model. We further find that, across all specifications, *Contdem* is statistically significant and negative when *SOLS Change* equals 1 and when it is 0.[27]

Regarding control variables, we find that, as expected, membership in trade agreements – both in the GATT/WTO and in Preferential Trade Agreements – is associated with smaller yearly changes in dyadic import patterns. Similarly, wealthy states experience less volatility in trade; both *State A's GDP* and *State B's GDP* are significantly negatively correlated with yearly change in imports. By contrast, economic turmoil in A correlates with greater changes in state A's imports from B, as does regime change in B. The end of the Cold War is also associated with new trading patterns. Counter to our expectations, countries' status as either an American or Soviet ally during the Cold War did not entail greater continuity in dyadic import patterns. Instead, indicators of alliances with the US and the USSR for both A and B are significantly positively correlated with changes in import volumes from B to A. There is mixed evidence on the role of domestic conflict in A and international conflict between A and B. Counter to what one would expect, domestic conflict in A is negatively

---

[27] Dropping cases of regime transition and limiting our examination to continuing democracies and continuing nondemocracies does not affect our conclusions. When we use the full sample of directed-dyads in the Gleditsch (2002) trade data, dropping only observations in which the source of import data changed from one year to the next, our results are also robust. Finally, our conclusions are substantively similar when we consider models that include both unit and year fixed effects and models without fixed effects, though there are some differences. In specifications with two-way fixed effects, the correlation between *SOLS Change* and *Changes in Import Patterns* in democracies is not statistically significant at conventional levels and the marginal effect of *SOLS Change* is significantly greater in nondemocracies than in democracies ($p < 0.05$). By contrast, without fixed effects, in the Basic and Control 1 models, *SOLS Change* is highly significant in both democracies and nondemocracies and the size of the marginal effect of *SOLS Change* in each of these samples is very similar. In the Control 2 model, *SOLS Change* is only significant for democracies and not for nondemocracies; there is no statistically significant difference in the two marginal effects.

Table 9 Change in dyadic import patterns, pooled models

	Basic	Control 1	Control 2
SOLS Change (A)	0.040**	0.042**	0.042**
	(0.009)	(0.009)	(0.009)
Continuing Democracy (A)	−0.163**	−0.107**	−0.070**
	(0.014)	(0.016)	(0.016)
Regime Transition (A)		−0.012	0.005
		(0.022)	(0.023)
US or USSR Cold War Ally (A)		0.169**	0.056**
		(0.012)	(0.014)
Domestic Conflict (A)		−0.017	−0.0416**
		(0.013)	(0.013)
Interstate Conflict (A–B)		0.270⁺	0.191
		(0.150)	(0.149)
End of Cold War		0.155**	0.189**
		(0.011)	(0.011)
Economic Turmoil		0.031**	0.042**
		(0.010)	(0.010)
Joint GATT/WTO Membership			−0.116**
			(0.014)
Joint PTA Membership			−0.135**
			(0.015)
SOLS Change (B)			−0.003
			(0.009)
Regime Transition (B)			0.057**
			(0.021)
US or USSR Cold War Ally (B)			0.066**
			(0.013)
Domestic Conflict (B)			0.071**
			(0.014)
GDP (A)			−0.074**
			(0.010)
GDP (B)			−0.042**
			(0.010)
Constant	0.982**	0.876**	3.536**
	(0.007)	(0.010)	(0.230)
N	401,492	394,101	375,707
Adjusted R^2	0.001	0.002	0.005
Directed-dyad FE	Yes	Yes	Yes

Note: Coefficients with robust SE clustered on the directed-dyad in parentheses. $+ p < 0.1$, $* p < 0.05$, $** p < 0.01$.

Table 10 Change in dyadic import patterns, interaction models

	Basic	**Control 1**	**Control 2**
SOLS Change (A)	0.067**	0.072**	0.060**
	(0.012)	(0.017)	(0.018)
Continuing Democracy (A)	–0.156**	–0.102**	–0.067**
	(0.014)	(0.016)	(0.016)
SOLS Change (A) × Continuing	–0.043*	–0.047*	–0.029
Democracy (A)	(0.019)	(0.020)	(0.021)
Regime Transition (A)		–0.030	–0.006
		(0.024)	(0.024)
US or USSR Cold War Ally (A)		0.168**	0.056**
		(0.012)	(0.014)
Domestic Conflict (A)		–0.017	–0.041**
		(0.013)	(0.013)
Interstate Conflict (A–B)		0.270[+]	0.192
		(0.150)	(0.149)
End of Cold War		0.155**	0.189**
		(0.011)	(0.011)
Economic Turmoil		0.031**	0.041**
		(0.010)	(0.010)
Joint GATT/WTO Membership			–0.116**
			(0.014)
Joint PTA Membership			–0.135**
			(0.015)
SOLS Change (B)			–0.003
			(0.009)
Regime Transition (B)			0.057**
			(0.021)
US or USSR Cold War Ally (B)			0.066**
			(0.013)
Domestic Conflict (B)			0.071**
			(0.014)
GDP (A)			–0.074**
			(0.010)
GDP (B)			–0.042**
			(0.010)
Constant	0.978**	0.874**	3.524**
	(0.007)	(0.010)	(0.230)
N	401,492	394,101	375,707

Table 10 (cont.)

	Basic	Control 1	Control 2
Adjusted. R^2	0.001	0.002	0.005
Directed-dyad FE	Yes	Yes	Yes

Note: Coefficients with robust SE clustered on the directed-dyad in parentheses. $+ p < 0.1$, $* p < 0.05$, $** p < 0.01$.

correlated with changes in import patterns, but this relationship is only statistically significant in the Control 2 model. In line with theoretical expectations, the correlation between interstate conflict and the dependent variable is positive, but it is only weakly significant in the Control 1 model ($p<0.1$) and not significant in the Control 2 model. Domestic conflict in State B, however, is strongly positively correlated with the change in import patterns, in line with theoretical expectations. There is no evidence of a systematic relationship between regime transition in A or SOLS changes in B and our dependent variable.

Overall, this analysis produces mixed results. Consistent with our expectations, we find evidence that leader transitions that bring to office new leaders with a different domestic supporting coalition than their predecessor lead to changes in a country's trading preferences. Counter to our expectations, SOLS changes appear to be systematically correlated with changes in import patterns not just in nondemocracies, but also in democracies. There is some evidence that SOLS changes in nondemocracies are associated with more sizable changes in import patterns than SOLS changes in democracies, but the evidence is not consistent on this point. Thus, we conclude that, in contrast to the three other foreign policy areas we examined, in trade, SOLS changes might prompt foreign policy change in both democracies and nondemocracies.

4.2 Comparing SOLS Changes to Other Types of Leader Transition

Our project focuses on the role of a particular type of leader transition – leader changes that bring to power a new leader who represents different interests and preferences than their predecessor – in prompting foreign policy change. A natural question to ask is whether SOLS changes really are distinct from leader changes in which the new and old leader share the same domestic support base. Thus, in this section, we examine the association of non-SOLS-change leader transitions, alongside SOLS changes, with each of our four dependent variables. We also consider the mode of leader transition – that is, whether it followed constitutional procedures (regular) or whether the leader assumed power through pathways outside the country's institutional rules, for example through a coup or foreign imposition (irregular). The mode of leader transition may be seen as a confounder of the effect of SOLS changes, especially in nondemocracies. To ensure that our finding on the association between SOLS change and foreign policy change is not simply capturing the effect of irregular leader transitions, we conduct analyses for each of our dependent variables that include a binary indicator of whether a leader assumed office through irregular means.

4.2.1 SOLS Changes and Non-SOLS-Change Leader Transitions

To contrast the relationship between SOLS changes and foreign policy change with the relationship between non-SOLS-change leader transitions and foreign policy change we focus on our pooled models. For each dependent variable, we create an *Other Leader Transition* dummy that parallels our SOLS change indicator but codes transitions in which the new leader and the old leader represent the same domestic groups. *SOLS Change* and *Other Leader Transition* are mutually exclusive. Here we review whether *Other Leader Transition* is correlated with foreign policy change in each of the four foreign policy domains of interest, how the inclusion of this additional parameter affects the statistical association between *SOLS Change* and foreign policy change, and whether the coefficients associated with these two forms of leader transition are statistically different. We present the full results tables in the web appendix.

In our analysis of alliance violation, we consistently find, across all three model specifications, that *Other Leader Transition* is not significantly correlated with the dependent variable, that *SOLS Change* continues to be significantly positively associated with a greater likelihood of alliance termination when *Other Leader Transition* is included in the model, and that the effect of *SOLS Change* is statistically different from that of *Other Leader Transition* (p<0.05). These results thus align with our expectation that when a new leader with a different domestic support base comes to power, changes in a country's alliance relationship are more likely than when a new leader represents the same interests and preferences as the predecessor.

In our analysis of UNGA voting, we find that, like SOLS changes, non-SOLS change leader transitions are significantly positively correlated with changes in a country's ideal point. Furthermore, the two coefficients, *SOLS Change* and *Other Leader Transition*, are very similar in size and not statistically different from one another. These patterns exist both in the Basic and the Control 1 specifications. It appears that in the area of UNGA voting, leader transitions, irrespective of whether they entail a change in source of leader support, are generally associated with foreign policy change.[28]

In our analysis of the sanctions sample that includes US cases, we find that neither *SOLS Change* nor *Other Leader Transition* are systematically correlated with sender capitulation; the two coefficients are also not statistically different from one another. When we drop US cases, across all three specifications, we find that non-SOLS-change leader transitions are not associated with sender capitulation, but *SOLS Change* remains statistically significant and positive. The coefficient of *SOLS Change* is also statistically different from that of *Other Leader Transition* (p<0.05). These findings thus support the idea that there is a difference between SOLS-change and non-SOLS-change leader transitions when it comes to sender decisions to capitulate.

Finally, with regard to changes in dyadic import patterns, we find, in the Basic and Control 1 specifications, that *Other Leader Transition* is significantly correlated with the dependent variable (p<0.01), that *SOLS Change* remains statistically significant (p<0.01), and that the effect of *SOLS Change* is not significantly different from that of *Other Leader Transition*. In the Control 2 specification, only *SOLS Change* is statistically significant (p<0.01) and its coefficient is significantly larger than that capturing other leader transitions (p<0.05). Findings in this issue area are thus mixed.

In summary, in two of our foreign policy areas – alliance termination and sanctions termination – we find that foreign policy change is systematically more likely when a leader transition brings about a change in domestic groups with sway over policymaking than when simply the identity of the leader changes. For trade, our findings are less clear; in some specifications, both SOLS changes and other leader transitions are associated with changes in dyadic imports. In our analysis of UNGA voting there is a significant relationship between foreign policy change and non-SOLS-change leader transitions. It is perhaps not surprising that either type of leader transition correlates with foreign policy change in this particular area. UNGA voting, after all, is the domain that we expect to have the fewest constraints, whether domestic or international, on executive decisionmaking; thus, change should generally be more likely in this area.

4.2.2 SOLS Changes and Irregular Leader Transitions

Unlike for non-SOLS-change leader transitions, our goal for the analysis of irregular leader transitions is not to assess whether the latter have an equally

---

[28] Here our findings deviate from our previous study (Mattes et al. 2015), where we found a significant difference in the estimated effects of *SOLS Change* and *Other Leader Transition*.

strong relationship with foreign policy change, but to determine whether some of the estimated effect of *SOLS Change* may be due to the mode of leader transition (i.e. whether the leader transition followed constitutional rules or not). Accounting for the mode of leader transition is arguably most important for nondemocracies, where we might otherwise conflate the effect of preference shocks with that of revolutions, coups, or other disruptive processes of leader change. As we argue elsewhere (Mattes et al. 2016), we are skeptical that the mode of leader transition per se leads to continuity or change in foreign policy. While it is plausible that a leader who attains office through a revolution or coup may be inclined to change their predecessor's policy, we argue that what actually leads to foreign policy change is likely the fact that the new leader's domestic support group is different from the predecessor's, rather than the revolution or coup event itself. Our tests try to disentangle these possibilities by running two sets of analyses: one in which we include SOLS change and irregular entry variables that vary independently of one another, and one in which we code irregular entry only when there was not also a SOLS change.

To identify irregular leader transitions, we rely on Archigos v.4.1 (Goemans et al. 2009), which covers all countries through 2015. Using Archigos's *Irregular Entry* variable, we create a dummy variable that is coded 1 when the new leader assumes office in an irregular manner or is imposed by another state. For the construction of this variable, we use the same operational rules as we used to create *SOLS Change* to identify when and for how long the effect of an irregular entry might manifest itself in each of our four foreign policy areas. We create two versions of this variable: 1) *Irregular* identifies every case of irregular leader transition, and 2) *Irregular Exclusive* is only coded 1 when there is an irregular leader transition that is not also accompanied by a SOLS change. In our analysis of the role of irregular transitions, we focus on our interaction models. This allows us to examine how the inclusion of a control variable for irregular leader transitions affects the relationship between SOLS changes and foreign policy change in both nondemocracies and democracies. As in the preceding section, we report results here but point the reader to the web appendix for tables.

In our sample of bilateral alliances, we code 136 observations as experiencing an irregular leader transition; most of them (84; 62%) are also accompanied by a SOLS change. We first rerun our interaction models, adding the *Irregular* variable. Across specifications, the coefficient of *Irregular* is positive and highly statistically significant, suggesting a strong systematic relationship with alliance violation. Furthermore, we find an attenuation of the association between SOLS changes and the dependent variable. Alliance abrogation is approximately twice as likely when a new leader with a different supporting coalition assumes office in a nondemocracy than when no SOLS change occurs, but this estimate is only significant in the Basic and Control 2 models ($p<0.05$). Across all three specifications, there is no evidence of a correlation between SOLS changes and alliance violation in democracies. Unlike in our models without *Irregular*, we do not find the estimated effects in democracies and nondemocracies to be statistically different from one another. These findings suggest that the coincidence of an irregular leader transition might account at least in part for the observed correlation between *SOLS Change* and *Alliance Violation*.

We next turn to our alternative measure of irregular leader transition, *Irregular Exclusive*. If the mode of leader transition has an effect on alliance violation independent of a co-occurring SOLS change, we should find this indicator, which captures irregular transitions that were not also SOLS changes, to be statistically significantly related to the dependent variable. Instead, what we find is that *Irregular Exclusive* is dropped from our models because it predicts the outcome perfectly – there are no instances of alliance violation when a leader who has the same domestic supporting coalition as their predecessor took power through irregular means. This finding is in line with our view that the mode of leader transition per se is unlikely to be a significant predictor of foreign policy change, but rather that it is the frequent co-occurrence of SOLS changes with irregular leader transitions that are associated with change in a country's alliance profile.

In our UNGA country-year data, there are 217 irregular leader transitions, with most (148; 68%) coinciding with SOLS changes. When we include *Irregular* in our interaction models, we find that this dummy variable is statistically significant in the Basic and Control 1 specifications. Furthermore, the inclusion of this variable strongly diminishes the correlation between *SOLS Change* and *UNGA Ideal Point Change* in nondemocracies. The marginal effect of *SOLS Change* when *Contdem* is equal to 0 is not statistically significant at conventional levels in either specification. As before, for democracies, we find no relationship between SOLS changes and yearly changes in how a country votes in the UNGA.

We probe these results by rerunning our analyses replacing *Irregular* with *Irregular Exclusive*. Irregular transitions that do not also coincide with SOLS changes are uncorrelated with UNGA vote change and the marginal effect of *SOLS Change* is positive and significant for nondemocracies in both specifications, as in our main analysis. These results again suggest that it is likely not the mode of transition per se that prompts foreign policy change, but rather that it is when irregular transitions coincide with preference shocks that we see UNGA vote change.

In our sanctions sample, irregular leader transitions are very rare. We only observe twenty-two sanctions-months in which *Irregular* is coded 1, with fourteen (64%) of these observations also coded as experiencing a SOLS change. The paucity of irregular leader changes, especially in combination with the low number of nondemocratic observations, makes formal statistical analysis questionable, but, for completeness, we examine what happens if we control for the mode of leader transition. *Irregular* is not significantly correlated with sanctions termination, and we continue to observe a positive statistically significant association between *SOLS Change* and *Sender Capitulation* in non-democracies across specifications and samples. There are no cases of sender capitulation that followed an irregular transition that did not also involve a SOLS change.

In our dyadic import data, 16,029 dyad-years are coded as experiencing an irregular leader transition in the previous year. Most of these (11,011; 69%) coincide with a SOLS change. Across models, *Irregular* is not statistically significant, while the correlation between *SOLS Change* and *Changes in Import Patterns* remains statistically significant for both nondemocracies and democracies. Interestingly, when we include *Irregular*, the marginal effect of *SOLS Change* in nondemocracies is significantly greater than in democracies. The results for *Irregular Exclusive* are similar.

In summary, it appears that across our four areas of foreign policy, to the extent that the mode of leader transition correlates with changes in a country's international behavior, much of this correlation is accounted for by the simul-taneous presence of SOLS changes. We believe that it is more likely that the presence or absence of overlap between the new and old leader's supporting coalitions predicts the mode of leader transition than that the reverse is true. Going forward, it may be informative to study the relationship between SOLS changes and irregular leader transitions. Future research could examine whether SOLS changes that coincide with irregular transitions of power signify the most significant breaks with a country's past interests and thus that these events portend the most significant redirection of a country's foreign policy.

4.3 Summarizing Across Four Areas of Foreign Policy

We have now considered the correlation between changes in SOLS and four different indicators of foreign policy change. Our four issues areas – alliances, UNGA voting, economic sanctions, and trade – span economic and security issues, vary in their domestic political salience and the breadth of domestic actors involved in decisionmaking, and include both policies that are supported by treaties and international organizations and those that are not. A consistent pattern emerges regarding our first hypothesis. Across all of these issue areas, we find that changes in the primary societal support base of leaders is associated with changes in foreign policy, although in the economic sanctions analysis this is only true once we drop the large portion of cases led by the United States. In at least two of these issue areas, we find that the same relationship does not hold for leadership changes that are not accompanied by a change in the source of leader support. Thus, there is significant evidence commensurate with our hypothesis that societal competition between groups with competing interests and ideologies impacts foreign policy, just as it impacts domestic policy.

We also hypothesized, however, that the effect of SOLS change on foreign policy change would be moderated by domestic political institutions, and in particular that we would see a weaker association between SOLS change and foreign policy change in democracies than in nondemocracies. In three of the four issue areas, we see evidence commensurate with this hypothesis. SOLS changes in nondemocracies are systematically associated with a higher risk of alliance violation and greater changes in UNGA ideal points; there is also evidence that SOLS changes in nondemocracies are linked to a higher probability of sanctions termination, but the low number of nondemocratic cases in that analysis makes us wary of drawing strong conclusions about nondemocracies. By contrast, for democracies – of which we have plenty of cases across all three foreign policy arenas – we find no systematic relationship between SOLS changes and alliance violation, UNGA vote change, or sanctions termination. Across these three foreign policy domains, there is also evidence to suggest that the magnitude of the effect of SOLS changes may be larger in nondemocracies than in democracies. In our trade analysis, however, SOLS changes are associated with change in dyadic import patterns in both democracies and nondemocracies. Given that trade is the area with the most salient distributional effects within societies (Milner and Tingley 2015), it is perhaps not surprising that this is the area in which SOLS changes systematically correlate with foreign policy change even in democracies. Variance in the strength of domestic distributional effects across issue areas likely affects the role SOLS changes play in the foreign policy of democratic states.

SOLS changes are much more common in democracies than in nondemocracies, but we fail to find a systematic relationship between them and foreign policy change in three of our four policy domains. This does not mean that SOLS changes may not, at times, lead to significant foreign policy change in any area of foreign policy, including in the areas of alliances, UNGA voting, and sanctions, but rather that they do not do so systematically. Our argument is not that democracies never change their foreign policies in response to changes in domestic interests; that would call into question principles of representation and accountability. Instead, we argue that because of institutional rules regarding leader selection and policymaking processes, foreign policy changes will be of smaller magnitude and will be more gradual, on average. This leads to less immediate uncertainty at any point in time about the future foreign policy of democracies. We readily acknowledge, however, that our empirical findings are based on historical data, and changes in the domestic politics of democracies may be underway that may affect these patterns in the future. In Section 5, we discuss what our theory leads us to expect going forward.

5 Looking Forward

As we write in 2021, recent leader transitions in countries as diverse as Burundi, the Dominican Republic, Bolivia, Moldova, Nepal, and the United States have spawned discussions about the extent to which the incoming leaders will depart from the foreign policies of their predecessors. In some cases, questions have arisen about how these leaders will position their countries relative to global and regional powers as well as international organizations, while in other cases, observers are interested to see whether these countries will more generally reverse the international isolation caused by their predecessors.

The goal of this Element is to shed light on the potential for foreign policy change resulting from leader transitions such as those noted earlier. We present and test a theory of domestically motivated foreign policy change that highlights both factors that propel change and factors that hamper it. In the following sections we review key insights from our theoretical argument and empirical conclusions. We then turn to the question of what the future may hold for democratic foreign policy stability, given widespread trends of polarization and democratic backsliding. We conclude with some final thoughts on the link between accountability and foreign policy continuity.

5.1 Argument, Evidence, and Contributions

A core element of our theory is the concept of Source of Leader Support (SOLS), which we have introduced as a new unit of analysis in the study of foreign policy. We have argued that just as groups within society with different interests and ideologies influence the domestic policies pursued by their countries, they also influence foreign policy. Even if international conditions remain largely unchanged, when new leaders come to power who rely on the support of different societal groups than their predecessors, they may have incentives to pursue new foreign policies. These incentives, however, vary with the rules of leader selection within polities; in democracies, leaders depend on large numbers of supporters to stay in power and there are incentives to accommodate actors outside a leader's SOLS. In democracies, chief executives also face significant policymaking barriers from constraining actors outside their SOLS in the legislature, bureaucracy, and judiciary. The logics of selection and policymaking led us to expect more consistent and larger foreign policy changes associated with SOLS changes in nondemocracies than democracies.

We evaluated this theory in four issue areas – alliances, UNGA voting, sanctions, and trade – that feature varying levels of domestic salience, domestic constraint, and international institutionalization. Across these very different issue areas we found consistent evidence that SOLS changes are associated with foreign policy change. In three of these areas – alliances, UNGA voting, and sanctions – we also found that this relationship is driven by nondemocracies; there was no systematic association between SOLS change in democracies and foreign policy change. The only issue area in which we found evidence of a correlation between SOLS change and foreign policy change in democracies is trade.

Our study thus highlights the domestic basis of foreign policy and speaks to the long-standing debate about whether democracies conduct more or less consistent foreign policies. By focusing on conditions under which domestic political interests have changed while controlling for international factors that also drive foreign policy, we provide evidence in line with the idea that foreign policy is a matter of competition among domestic interests and ideologies, just as domestic policy is. At the same time, while changes in domestic interests with sway over the leader are more common in democracies than nondemocracies, they also seem to be less systematically associated with foreign policy change and less consequential for foreign policy in democracies. Democracies appear to be more consistent in their foreign policies in such diverse areas as military alliances, voting at the UNGA, and economic sanctions, both at times when SOLS changes occur and when they do not. The area of trade, however, forms an exception: here there appears to be potential for democracies to change their policies when leaders with different domestic supporting coalitions come to office. Overall, we conclude that, across the foreign policy areas under examination, democracies were never more likely and mostly less likely to experience significant foreign policy change than nondemocracies.

5.2 Challenges to Foreign Policy Stability in Democracies

As we bring this Element to a close, we are aware that recent developments around the world appear to challenge the idea that democracies enjoy an advantage in conducting a stable foreign policy, as compared to nondemocracies. In particular, the foreign policy changes wrought by former US President Trump appear inconsistent with the claim of democratic stability. In his four years in office, President Trump undid many of his predecessor's commitments, including the Trans-Pacific Partnership (TPP), the Paris Climate Accord, and the Iran Nuclear Deal; he deviated from established US policy positions, for example by recognizing Jerusalem as the capital of Israel; and he more generally moved the United States away from multilateralism, even expressing support for a more isolationist stance, as captured in his slogan "America First!"

How can we understand the Trump presidency in light of our theoretical argument and the empirical evidence? While President Trump clearly broke with many of his predecessor's foreign policies, there is variation in which policies saw more and less disruption. Trump often railed against existing US alliances and engaged in rhetoric that seemed to undermine them, but he did not make any attempt to withdraw from those alliances – and, in fact, Congress preemptively voted its overwhelming support for maintaining the US commitment to NATO.[29] While Trump rolled back some changes to US sanctions on Cuba that his predecessor had loosened, Congress acted to stop Trump from ending sanctions against Russia.[30] In the area of trade, Trump made more significant foreign policy changes – for example, through the renegotiation of NAFTA to the USMCA. All of this is consistent with our theory and findings. Trump's SOLS was different from the SOLS of his predecessor, and his new coalition had different interests and ideological commitments. It is therefore not surprising that he sought to change the direction of US foreign policy. At the same time, he found it challenging to overcome constraints placed upon him by Congress, the bureaucracy, and the courts. The area in which he was most successful was the domestically salient issue of trade, which is the only area in which we found SOLS changes in democracies to be systematically associated with change in foreign policy outcomes.

Furthermore, we do not claim that SOLS changes in democracies never lead to foreign policy change, but simply that they don't do so systematically, as they seem to in nondemocracies. Sometimes SOLS changes in democracies have led to significant foreign policy change, such as when the new West German Social Democratic Chancellor Brandt pursued his *Ostpolitik* after years of German *Westbindung*, or when French President De Gaulle pursued a foreign policy of

---

[29] On July 10, 2018, the Senate voted 97–2 in favor of a nonbinding resolution in support of NATO, and on January 22, 2019, the House of Representatives passed H.R. 676, known as the NATO Support Act, by a vote of 357–22.

[30] In July, 2017, the House voted 419–3 and the Senate voted 98–2 to impose new sanctions on Russia and to prevent Trump from relaxing sanctions on Russia without Congressional review.

greater independence from the United States and the United Kingdom. But this is not the norm. It is possible that President Trump's actions may be seen in this light – as an aberration – but it is also possible that his presidency signals a more profound change in how democracies can be expected to conduct their foreign policies in the future.

Beyond Donald Trump's presidency looms the larger question of whether democracies may be experiencing domestic political changes that will affect their ability to be reliable partners and steadfast adversaries internationally. Two phenomena – polarization and democratic backsliding – deserve particular consideration in this context. In the following sections we use our theoretical framework to analyze their implications for foreign policy consistency.

5.2.1 Polarization

Traditionally, polarization has been understood as a split into different camps that embrace increasingly extreme ideological positions and/or as the sorting of individuals into distinct partisan camps with few cross-cutting cleavages (Hetherington 2009; Levendusky 2009). This can happen at the elite level, the mass level, or both. More recently, scholars have highlighted a distinct dimension of polarization – "affective polarization" – whereby different camps develop a deep antipathy toward one another (for a review, see Iyengar et al. 2019). The phenomenon of polarization has been studied extensively in the US context, but there is evidence that other Western democracies also experience significant levels of polarization (Lupu 2015; Gidron, Adams, and Horne 2020; Reiljan 2020). This polarization poses a danger not only to the quality of domestic governance in democracies, but also to their foreign policies (Schultz 2017; Myrick 2018). We argue that polarization may undermine both the selection and the policymaking mechanisms that our theory identifies as inducing democratic stability.

With regard to the selection mechanism, polarization at the level of the masses is of particular concern. To understand why, it is useful to examine how mass polarization may affect the various logics that we highlighted in Section 2.2.1. We argue that when leaders have a large SOLS, a) there is an increased likelihood of overlap in the SOLS of successive leaders, b) consecutive leaders may have an incentive to appeal to the median voter, c) there is greater heterogeneity in each leader's SOLS, and d) leaders are incentivized to produce public goods over private ones.

Assuming that the size of leaders' SOLS remains constant, polarization should not affect the likelihood of overlap between two consecutive leaders' SOLS (a), and greater disagreement among members of the leader's SOLS may indeed increase heterogeneity and make departure from the status quo harder (c). However, a clear danger is that mass ideological polarization undermines the pull toward moderate policies under the median voter theorem (b). When there are few centrists, leaders and their parties have weakened incentives to appeal to the median voter. Instead, they may focus their electoral strategy on mobilizing their base for turnout. Some have argued that partisan turnout strategies are becoming more relevant – and median voter dynamics less relevant – not only in the United States, but also in some European countries, as voter turnout has been declining there in recent years (Fraenkel 2016). If centrist policies become less attractive, swinging back and forth between extreme positions becomes more likely as governments change. In the presence of polarization, it should also be more likely that different ideological camps espouse preferences for different public goods, leading to a demand for different policies (d). We also argue that maintaining the legitimacy of democratic processes requires treating political losers gently. Under affective polarization in particular, winners may have reduced incentives to court election losers; given the strong antipathy between factions, leaders who attempt to do so could be penalized by their SOLS. Affective polarization is arguably a particularly significant challenge for foreign policy consistency: to the extent that voters dislike and distrust the other side, they may support and even demand a new leader's abrogation of foreign policies previously embraced by a predecessor with a different SOLS.

As we argue in Section 2.2.2, in democracies constraining actors can step in to curtail a leader's foreign policy endeavors. Polarization per se should not affect the number of political actors that have the *ability* to constrain leaders, but it does affect these actors' *willingness* to do so. For the policymaking mechanism, it is elite rather than mass polarization that is of concern. The effect of elite polarization depends on the preference distribution across constraining actors in the legislature, bureaucracy, and judiciary. When constraining actors share the leader's SOLS or are members of the leader's SOLS, they should be less likely to seek to restrict the leader (Tsebelis 2002). In fact, polarization should reinforce the unwillingness to check a leader who comes from the same camp. But if the distribution of preferences among constraining actors is such that they deviate from those of the leader's SOLS, then we should expect increased efforts to restrain the leader. Under divided government or when the bureaucracy or courts are dominated by individuals affiliated with a different SOLS, leaders may have limited options for foreign policy change.

A complicating factor is that polarization may delegitimize constraint in the eyes of a leader's SOLS. This opens the possibility for leaders to seek to insulate themselves from pressure by constraining actors that represent different SOLS.

For example, in the US context, Schultz (2017) warns that polarization incentivizes US presidents to rely on executive agreements rather than treaties. Greater reliance on policy tools that are under the unilateral control of the leader, in turn, creates greater leeway for their successors to abandon these commitments, thus undermining foreign policy stability.

Scholars have started to examine the effects of polarization on the international behavior of states. Schultz (2017) discusses the myriad complications polarization causes for American foreign policy. Building on his study, Myrick (2018) provides evidence that the greater the ideological split with the predecessor, the more likely new leaders in democracies were to abandon existing policies. By Myrick's account, polarization may explain some of the heterogeneity that we observe historically in democracies: leadership change and SOLS changes are not consistently related to foreign policy change, but occasionally there are moments of sharp departures from the status quo, and these may occur when there is a stark ideological split between the old and new leader. Our arguments about selection and policymaking provide additional theoretical traction to understand the potentially pernicious effect of polarization on foreign policy stability in democracies going forward.

5.2.2 Democratic Backsliding

In addition to polarization, another contemporary phenomenon relevant to the question of stability in democratic foreign policy is democratic backsliding. In recent years, a host of current and former democracies – such as India, Turkey, Hungary, Poland, Bolivia, Venezuela, and the United States – have experienced incremental declines in democratic governance.[31] Research on democratic backsliding is still relatively new, and there remain debates about what exactly constitutes backsliding (Hyde 2020). Much of the existing work focuses on how powerholders have weakened mechanisms for vertical accountability: by impeding voters' participation in elections, by making elections less competitive through gerrymandering or outright fraud, and by undermining the ability of citizens to access information that would allow them to evaluate leaders and their policies (Waldner and Lust 2018; Hyde 2020). Scholars have also pointed to instances of "executive aggrandizement," whereby leaders have curtailed horizontal accountability by undermining the powers of the opposition in the legislature, by diminishing judicial independence, and/or by weakening the bureaucracy (Bermeo 2016). Both of these facets of democratic backsliding

---

[31] Cross-national studies by Meyerrose (2020) and Lührmann and Lindberg (2019) point to a broader trend of democratic backsliding and autocratization.

should be expected to have consequences not just for domestic governance but also for foreign policy.

The consequence of limiting voter participation in elections and making elections less competitive is that the size of the selectorate in democracies shrinks and, as a result, leaders require a smaller SOLS to hold office. We do not necessarily expect there to be less overlap in the SOLS of two successive leaders in this case, given that both leaders draw support from the same selectorate that has systematically excluded particular societal groups. However, based on our selection mechanism, we expect that the fact that leaders rely on smaller SOLS encourages foreign policy change in different ways: smaller SOLS may be more homogenous, lowering the likelihood that deadlock among the leader's supporters prevents a change in the status quo; and, with a smaller SOLS, delivering private goods as opposed to public ones becomes more attractive, leading to a greater likelihood that two consecutive leaders choose different policies based on what serves them best with their respective supporters. In addition, if political losers can be marginalized in future elections, there is no need to be concerned about their support for the system.

Executive aggrandizement, in turn, undermines the ability of constraining actors to limit leaders' discretion over foreign policy, and thus removes some of the brakes democratic systems of governance have in place to ensure policy continuity. Where leaders skirt checks by the legislature (e.g. by refusing to provide information about and justification for government policy), undercut the independence of courts (e.g. by exclusively appointing justices that are ideologically aligned), and/or weaken the bureaucracy (e.g. by cutting the number of public servants and/or penalizing perceived disloyalty), constraining actors are deprived of their power to influence the approval, implementation, and enforcement of policy. As a result, leaders who may want to change policy, including foreign policy, are in an excellent position to do so.

Unlike for polarization, we are not aware of studies that examine the effect of democratic backsliding on foreign policymaking. However, the theoretical mechanisms of selection and policymaking that we present in this Element may afford scholars some traction to understand the likely foreign policy implications of democratic backsliding, just as these mechanisms might help shed more light on the foreign policy effects of polarization. As we write this Element, much of the political – and political science – discourse bemoans the polarization and democratic backsliding that can be observed in many formerly robust democracies. These developments pose twin challenges not only for the quality of domestic governance in democracies but also for their foreign policy. Whether democratic foreign policy will become less stable going forward depends, in large part, on whether these domestic political processes accelerate, settle, or recede.

5.3 Final Thoughts

Democratic governance is based on accountability to constituents. Going back at least to de Tocqueville, many have wondered if this accountability makes democracy unsuitable to strong foreign relations. Deterrence, compellence, and long-term cooperation all require the ability of countries to make long-term commitments to policies that will extend beyond one leader.

Our argument helps to allay concerns about the stability of democratic foreign policy without undermining democratic accountability. First, we argue that the preferences of constituents, based on their interests and ideologies, are crucial to the policy choices of leaders. Our theory focuses on domestic competition over interests and ideologies as a key building block of foreign policy behavior. We then claim that because leaders have to take into account the preferences of a very large number of supporters in democracies, there typically is less variance in the policies pursued. Because leaders in nondemocracies are accountable to a small number of constituents, that accountability can lead to dramatic changes in the policy favored by one leader's SOLS to the next. Accountability to a broad set of interests is not incompatible with stability. In fact, it is leader accountability in nondemocracies that makes consistent foreign policy challenging.

Second, we argue that the policymaking processes in democracies create constraints on policy change. Because actors outside a leader's SOLS may have influence in the legislature, the courts, or the bureaucracy, chief executives have to pursue policies that are able to gain significant support outside the leader's SOLS. Essentially, this creates accountability not only to the leader's SOLS, but some accountability to those outside the leader's SOLS as well. Again, this increases the likelihood of consistency in policy, as a function of accountability rather than in opposition to it.

In conclusion, we argue that the broad accountability of democratic leaders encourages the policy stability that is central to democracies' ability to make credible long-term commitments and thus reap the benefits of effective cooperation with friends and deterrence of adversaries. By contrast, the accountability of nondemocratic leaders exclusively to small groups allows wide swings in international behavior. To the extent that polarization and democratic backsliding weaken democratic accountability, this could have influence not only on domestic politics, but also on international order. This is especially true if the foreign policies of our most influential world powers become less stable and predictable.

References

Abbott, K. W. and Snidal, D. 1998. Why states act through formal international organizations. *Journal of Conflict Resolution*, **42**(1), 3–32.

Adams, J. and Somer-Topcu, Z. 2009. Moderate now, win votes later: The electoral consequences of parties' policy shifts in 25 postwar democracies. *The Journal of Politics*, **71**(2), 678–692.

Aldrich, J. H., Gelpi, C., Feaver, P., Reifler, J., and Sharp, K. T. 2006. Foreign policy and the electoral connection. *Annual Review of Political Science*, **9**, 477–502.

Almond, G. A. 1950. *The American People and Foreign Policy*. New York: Harcourt, Brace, and Company.

Anderson, C., Blais, A., Bowler, S., Donovan, T., and Listhaug, O. 2005. *Losers' Consent: Elections and Democratic Legitimacy*. Oxford: Oxford University Press.

Baier, S. L. and Bergstrand, J. H. 2007. Do free trade agreements actually increase members' international trade? *Journal of International Economics*, **71**(1), 72–95.

Bailey, M. A., Strezhnev, A., and Voeten, E. 2017. Estimating dynamic state preferences from United Nations voting data. *Journal of Conflict Resolution*, **61**(2), 430–456.

Bapat, N. A. and Morgan, T. C. 2009. Multilateral versus unilateral sanctions reconsidered: A test using new data. *International Studies Quarterly*, **53**(4), 1075–1094.

Barnhart, J. N., Trager, R. F., Saunders, E. N., and Dafoe, A. 2020. The suffragist peace. *International Organization*, **74**(4), 633–670.

Bearce, D. H. 2003. Societal preferences, partisan agents, and monetary policy outcomes. *International Organization*, **57**(2), 373–410.

Berinsky, A. J. 2007. Assuming the costs of war: Events, elites, and American public support for military conflict. *The Journal of Politics*, **69**(4), 975–997.

Bermeo, N. 2016. On democratic backsliding. *Journal of Democracy*, **27**(1), 5–19.

Black, D. 1948. On the rationale of group decision-making. *Journal of Political Economy*, **56**(1), 23–34.

Brazys, S. and Panke, D. 2017. Why do states change positions in the United Nations General Assembly? *International Political Science Review*, **38**(1), 70–84.

Bueno De Mesquita, B. and Siverson, R. M. 1995. War and the survival of political leaders: A comparative study of regime types and political accountability. *American Political Science Review*, **89**(4), 841–855.

Bueno De Mesquita, B., Smith, A., Siverson, R. M., and Morrow, J. D. 2003. *The Logic of Political Survival*. Cambridge: MIT Press.

Bunce, V. 1980. Changing leaders and changing policies: The impact of elite succession on budgetary priorities in democratic countries. *American Journal of Political Science*, **24**(3), 373–395.

Bunce, V. and Echols III, J. M. 1978. Power and policy in communist systems: The problem of incrementalism. *The Journal of Politics*, **40**(4), 911–932.

Canes-Wrone, B. Howell, W. G., and Lewis, D. E. 2008. Toward a broader understanding of presidential power: A reevaluation of the two presidencies thesis. *The Journal of Politics*, **70**(1), 1–16.

Carter, D. B. and Signorino, C. S. 2010. Back to the future: Modeling time dependence in binary data. *Political Analysis*, **18**(3), 271–292.

Carter, D. B. and Stone, R. W. 2015. Democracy and multilateralism: The case of vote buying in the UN General Assembly. *International Organization*, **69**(1), 1–33.

Chiozza, G. and Goemans, H. E. 2011. *Leaders and International Conflict*. Cambridge: Cambridge University Press.

Colgan, J. D. 2013. Domestic revolutionary leaders and international conflict. *World Politics*, **65**(4), 656–690.

Croco, S. E. 2011. The decider's dilemma: Leader culpability, war outcomes, and domestic punishment. *American Political Science Review*, **105**(3): 457–477.

Davis, D. R. and Moore, W. H. 1997. Ethnicity matters: Transnational ethnic alliances and foreign policy behavior. *International Studies Quarterly*, **41**(1), 171–184.

De Tocqueville, A. 1835. *Democracy in America*, trans. George Lawrence, ed. J. P. Mayer. Garden City, NY: Doubleday & Co.

Downs, A. 1957. *An Economic Theory of Democracy*. New York: Columbia University Press.

Dür, A., Baccini, L., and Elsig, M. 2014. The design of international trade agreements: Introducing a new dataset. *The Review of International Organizations*, **9**(3), 353–375.

Edry, J., Johnson, J., and Leeds, B. A. 2021. Threats at home and abroad: Interstate war, civil war, and alliance formation. *International Organization*, **75**(3), 837–857.

Erikson, R. S., MacKuen, M. B., and Stimson, J. A. 2002. *The Macro Polity*. Cambridge: Cambridge University Press

Ezrow, L. 2005. Are moderate parties rewarded in multiparty systems? A pooled analysis of Western European elections, 1984–1998. *European Journal of Political Research*, **44**(6), 1–19.

Foakes, J. 2015. Foreign affairs in national courts: The role of the executive certificate. Chatham House Briefing.

Fordham, B. O. 1998. Economic interests, party, and ideology in early Cold War era US foreign policy. *International Organization*, **52**(2), 359–396.

Fordham, B. O. 2019. The domestic politics of world power: Explaining debates over the United States battleship fleet, 1890–91. *International Organization*, **73**(2), 435–468.

Fraenkel, J. 2016. The death of the median voter. *The Interpreter*. Available at www.lowyinstitute.org/the-interpreter/death-median-voter.

Franklin, M. N., Mackie, T. T., and Valen, H. 1992. *Electoral Change: Responses to Evolving Social and Attitudinal Structures in Western Countries*. Cambridge: Cambridge University Press.

Frieden, J. 1988. Sectoral conflict and foreign economic policy, 1914–1940. *International Organization*, **42**(1), 59–90.

Fuhrmann, M. 2020. When do leaders free-ride? Business experience and contributions to collective defense. *American Journal of Political Science*, **64**(2), 416–431.

Gandhi, J. and Przeworski, A. 2006. Cooperation, cooptation, and rebellion under dictatorships. *Economics & Politics*, **18**(1), 1–26.

Gartzke, E. and Gleditsch, K. S. 2004. Why democracies may actually be less reliable allies. *American Journal of Political Science*, **48**(4), 775–795.

Gaubatz, K. T. 1996. Democratic states and commitment in international relations. *International Organization*, **50**(1), 109–139.

Geddes, B. 2003. *Paradigms and Sand Castles: Theory Building and Research Design in Comparative Politics*. Ann Arbor: University of Michigan Press.

Geddes, B., Wright, J., and Frantz, E. 2014. Autocratic breakdown and regime transitions: A new data set. *Perspectives on Politics*, **12**(2), 313–331.

Geddes, B., Wright, J., and Frantz, E. 2018. *How Dictatorships Work: Power, Personalization, and Collapse*. Cambridge: Cambridge University Press.

Gehlbach, S., Sonin, K., and Svolik, M. W. 2016. Formal models of nondemocratic politics. *Annual Review of Political Science*, **19**, 565–584.

Gidron, N., Adams, J., and Horne, W. 2020. *American Affective Polarization in Comparative Perspective*. Cambridge: Cambridge University Press.

Gleditsch, K. S. 2002. Expanded trade and GDP data. *Journal of Conflict Resolution*, **46**(5), 712–724.

Goemans, H. E., Gleditsch, K. S., and Chiozza, G. 2009. Introducing Archigos: A dataset of political leaders. *Journal of Peace Research*, **46**(2), 269–283.

Goldgeier, J. and Saunders, E. N. 2018. The unconstrained presidency: Checks and balances eroded long before Trump. *Foreign Affairs*, **97**(5), 144–156.

Guisinger, A. 2017. *American Opinion on Trade: Preferences Without Politics.* Oxford: Oxford University Press.

Guisinger, A. and Saunders, E. N. 2017. Mapping the boundaries of elite cues: How elites shape mass opinion across international issues. *International Studies Quarterly*, **61**(2), 425–441.

Haas, M. L. 2005. *The Ideological Origins of Great Power Politics, 1789–1989.* Ithaca: Cornell University Press.

Haftendorn, H. 2006. *Coming of Age: German Foreign Policy since 1945.* Lanham: Rowman & Littlefield Publishers.

Hagan, J. D. 1993. *Political Opposition and Foreign Policy in Comparative Perspective.* Boulder: Lynne Rienner Publishers.

Haggard, S. 1990. P*athways from the Periphery: The Politics of Growth in the Newly Industrializing Countries.* Ithaca: Cornell University Press.

Haney, P. J. and Vanderbush, W. 1999. The role of ethnic interest groups in US foreign policy: The case of the Cuban American National Foundation. *International Studies Quarterly*, **43**(2), 341–361.

Helfer, L. R. 2019. Treaty exit and intrabranch conflict at the interface of international and domestic law in *The Oxford Handbook of Comparative Foreign Relations Law.* Oxford: Oxford University Press.

Helmke, G. and Rosenbluth, F. 2009. Regimes and the rule of law: Judicial independence in comparative perspective. *Annual Review of Political Science*, **12**, 345–366.

Hetherington, M. J. 2009. Review article: Putting polarization in perspective. *British Journal of Political Science*, **39**(2), 413–448.

Holbrook, T. M. and McClurg, S. C. 2005. The mobilization of core supporters: Campaigns, turnout, and electoral composition in United States presidential elections. *American Journal of Political Science*, **49**(4): 689–703.

Holsti, O. R. 2006. *Making American Foreign Policy.* New York: Taylor & Francis.

Horowitz, M. C., Stam, A. C., and Ellis, C. M. 2015. *Why Leaders Fight.* Cambridge: Cambridge University Press.

Huber, J. D. and Shipan, C. R. 2002. *Deliberate Discretion? The Institutional Foundations of Bureaucratic Autonomy.* Cambridge: Cambridge University Press.

Hurwitz, J. and Peffley, M. 1987. How are foreign policy attitudes structured? A hierarchical model. *The American Political Science Review*, **81**(4), 1099–1120.

Hyde, S. D. 2020. Democracy's backsliding in the international environment. *Science*, **369**(6508), 1192–1196.

Hyde, S. D. and Saunders, E. N. 2020. Recapturing regime type in international relations: Leaders, institutions, and agency space. *International Organization*, **74**(2), 363–395.

Inglehart, R. 1997. *Modernization and Postmodernization: Cultural, Economic, and Political Change in 43 Societies.* Princeton: Princeton University Press.

Iyengar, S., Lelkes, Y., Levendusky, M., Malhotra, N., and Westwood, S. J. 2019. The origins and consequences of affective polarization in the United States. *Annual Review of Political Science*, **22**, 129–146.

Jensen, N. and McGillivray, F. 2005. Federal institutions and multinational investors: Federalism, government credibility, and foreign direct investment. *International Interactions*, **31**(4), 303–325.

Kaarbo, J., Lantis, J. S., and Beasley, R. K. 2012. The analysis of foreign policy in comparative perspective in J. S. Lantis, J. Kaarbo, R. K. Beasley, and M. T. Snarr (eds.), *Foreign Policy in Comparative Perspective: Domestic and International Influences on State Behavior.* Washington DC: SAGE Publications, 1–23.

Kaempfer, W. H. and Lowenberg, A. D. 2007. The political economy of economic sanctions in T. Sandler and K. Hartley (eds.), *Handbook of Defense Economics: Defense in a Globalized World*, **2**. Amsterdam: Elsevier Science & Technology, 867–911.

Karp, J. A., Banducci, S. A., and Bowler, S. 2008. Getting out the vote: Party mobilization in a comparative perspective. *British Journal of Political Science* **38**(1), 91–112.

Kertzer, J. D. and Zeitzoff, T. 2017. A bottom-up theory of public opinion about foreign policy. *American Journal of Political Science*, **61**(3), 543–558.

King, G., Tomz, M., and Wittenberg, J. 2000. Making the most of statistical analyses: Improving interpretation and presentation. *American Journal of Political Science*, **44**(2), 347–361.

King, K. L. and Meernik, J. 1999. The Supreme Court and the powers of the executive: The adjudication of foreign policy. *Political Research Quarterly*, **52**(4), 801–824.

Klingemann, H. D., Hofferbert, R. I., and Budge, I. 1994. *Parties, Policies, and Democracy.* Boulder: Westview Press.

Koremenos, B., Lipson, C. and Snidal, D. 2001. The rational design of international institutions. *International Organization*, **55**(4), 761–799.

Krasner, S. D. 1972. Are bureaucracies important? (or Allison Wonderland). *Foreign Policy*, **7**, 159–179.

Krcmaric, D., Nelson, S. C., and Roberts, A. 2020. Studying leaders and elites: The personal biography approach. *Annual Review of Political Science*, **23**, 133–151.

Krustev, V. L. and Morgan, T. C. 2011. Ending economic coercion: Domestic politics and international bargaining. *Conflict Management and Peace Science*, **28**(4), 351–376.

Leeds, B. A. and Anac, S. 2005. Alliance institutionalization and alliance performance. *International Interactions*, **31**(3), 183–202.

Leeds, B. A., Mattes, M., and Vogel, J. S. 2009. Interests, institutions, and the reliability of international commitments. *American Journal of Political Science*, **53**(2), 461–476.

Leeds, B. A., Ritter, J., Mitchell, S., and Long, A. 2002. Alliance treaty obligations and provisions, 1815–1944. *International Interactions*, **28**(3), 237–260.

Leeds, B. A. and Savun, B. 2007. Terminating alliances: Why do states abrogate agreements? *The Journal of Politics*, **69**(4), 1118–1132.

Levendusky, M. 2009. *The Partisan Sort: How Liberals became Democrats and Conservatives Became Republicans*. Chicago: University of Chicago Press.

Li, Q. and Vashchilko, T. 2010. Dyadic military conflict, security alliances, and bilateral FDI flows. *Journal of International Business Studies*, **41**(5), 765–782.

Lippmann, W. 1955. *Essays in the Public Philosophy*. Boston: Little, Brown, and Company.

Lipset, S. R. and Rokkan, S. 1967. Cleavage structures, party systems, and voter alignments: An introduction in S. M. Lipset and S. R. Rokkan (eds.), *Party Systems and Voter Alignments: Cross-national Perspectives*. New York : Free Press, 1–61.

Lipson, C. 2003. *Reliable Partners: How Democracies Have Made a Separate Peace*. Princeton: Princeton University Press.

Lobell, S. E. 2004. Politics and national security: The battles for Britain. *Conflict Management and Peace Science*, **21**(4), 269–286.

Lührmann, A. and Lindberg, S. I. 2019. A third wave of autocratization is here: What is new about it? *Democratization*, **26**(7), 1095–1113.

Lupu, N. 2015. Party polarization and mass partisanship: A comparative perspective. *Political Behavior*, **37**(2), 331–356.

Magaloni, B. 2008. Credible power-sharing and the longevity of authoritarian rule. *Comparative Political Studies*, **41**(4–5), 715–741.

Mansfield, E. D. and Bronson, R. 1997. Alliances, preferential trading arrangements, and international trade. *The American Political Science Review*, **91**(1), 94–107.

Mansfield, E. D. and Reinhardt, E. 2008. International institutions and the volatility of international trade. *International Organization*, **62**(4), 621–652.

Maoz, Z. and Russett, B. 1993. Normative and structural causes of the decentralized peace, 1946–1986. *American Political Science Review*, **87**(3), 914–924.

Marshall, M. G., Jaggers, K. and Gurr, T. R. 2012. *Polity IV Project: Dataset Users' Manual*. College Park: University of Maryland. Available at http://www.systemicpeace.org/polityproject.html.

Martin, L. L. 2000. *Democratic Commitments: Legislatures and International Cooperation*. Princeton: Princeton University Press.

Mattes, M. 2012. Democratic reliability, precommitment of successor governments, and the choice of alliance commitment. *International Organization*, **66**(1), 153–172.

Mattes, M., Leeds, B. A. and Carroll, R. 2015. Leadership turnover and foreign policy change: Societal interests, domestic institutions, and voting in the United Nations. *International Studies Quarterly*, **59**(2), 280–290.

Mattes, M., Leeds, B. A. and Matsumura, N. 2016. Measuring change in source of leader support: The CHISOLS dataset. *Journal of Peace Research*, **53**(2), 259–267.

Mattiacci, E. Forthcoming. *Volatile States in International Politics*. Oxford: Oxford University Press.

McDonald, M. D. and Budge, I. 2005. *Elections, Parties, Democracy: Conferring the Median Mandate*. Oxford: Oxford University Press.

McGillivray, F. and Smith, A. 2008. *Punishing the Prince: A Theory of Interstate Relations, Political Institutions, and Leader Change*. Princeton: Princeton University Press.

McGillivray, F. and Stam, A. C. 2004. Political institutions, coercive diplomacy, and the duration of economic sanctions. *Journal of Conflict Resolution*, **48**(2), 154–172.

Meyerrose, A. M. 2020. The unintended consequences of democracy promotion: International organizations and democratic backsliding. *Comparative Political Studies*, **53**(10–11), 1547–1581.

Milner, H. V. 1997. *Interests, Institutions, and Information: Domestic Politics and International Relations*. Princeton: Princeton University Press.

Milner, H. V. and Judkins, B. 2004. Partisanship, trade policy, and globalization: Is there a left–right divide on trade policy? *International Studies Quarterly*, **48**(1), 95–119.

Milner, H. V. and Tingley, D. 2015. *Sailing the Water's Edge: The Domestic Politics of American Foreign Policy*. Princeton: Princeton University Press.

Moon, B. E. 1985. Consensus or compliance? Foreign-policy change and external dependence. *International Organization*, **39**(2), 297–329.

Moosa, H. and Abi-Habib M. 2018. Fears of Maldives crisis ease after president concedes election loss. *New York Times*, www.nytimes.com/2018/09/24/world/asia/maldives-presidential-election-ibrahim-mohamed-solih.html.

Moravcsik, A. 1997. Taking preferences seriously: A liberal theory of international politics. *International Organization*, **51**(4), 513–553.

Morgan, T. C., Bapat, N. and Krustev, V. 2009. The threat and imposition of economic sanctions, 1971 – 2000. *Conflict Management and Peace Science*, **26**(1), 92–110.

Myrick, R. 2018. Towards the extremes: The impact of partisan polarization on international cooperation. Working paper.

Narizny, K. 2003. Both guns and butter, or neither: Class interests in the political economy of rearmament. *American Political Science Review*, **97** (2), 203–220.

Narizny, K. 2007. *The Political Economy of Grand Strategy*. Ithaca: Cornell University Press.

Page, B. I. and Shapiro, R. Y. 1982. Changes in Americans' policy preferences, 1935–1979. *Public Opinion Quarterly*, **46**(1), 24–42.

Rai, K. B. 1972. Foreign policy and voting in the UN General Assembly. *International Organization*, **26**(3), 589–594.

Rathbun, B. C. 2004. *Partisan Interventions: European Party Politics and Peace Enforcement in the Balkans*. Ithaca: Cornell University Press.

Rathbun, B. C., Kertzer, J. D., Reifler, J., Goren, P. and Scotto, T. J. 2016. Taking foreign policy personally: Personal values and foreign policy attitudes. *International Studies Quarterly*, **60**(1), 124–137.

Reiljan, A. 2020. 'Fear and loathing across party lines'(also) in Europe: Affective polarisation in European party systems. *European Journal of Political Research*, **59**(2), 376–396.

Risse-Kappen, T. 1991. Public opinion, domestic structure, and foreign policy in liberal democracies. *World Politics*, **43**(4), 479–512.

Rogowski, R. 1989. *Commerce and Coalitions: How Trade Affects Domestic Political Alignments*. Princeton: Princeton University Press.

Rosati, J. A. 1981. Developing a systematic decision-making framework: Bureaucratic politics in perspective. *World Politics*, **33**(2), 234–252.

Saunders, E. N. 2011. *Leaders at War: How Presidents Shape Military Interventions*. Ithaca: Cornell University Press.

Saunders, E. N. 2015. War and the inner circle: Democratic elites and the politics of using force. *Security Studies*, **24**(3), 466–501.

Saunders, E. N. 2017. No substitute for experience: Presidents, advisers, and information in group decision making. *International Organization*, **71**(S1), S219–S247.

Schultz, K. A. 2005. The politics of risking peace: Do hawks or doves deliver the olive branch? *International Organization*, **59**(1), 1–38.

Schultz, K. A. 2017. Perils of polarization for US foreign policy. *The Washington Quarterly*, **40**(4), 7–28.

Simmons, B. A. 1994. *Who Adjusts? Domestic Sources of Foreign Economic Policy During the Interwar Years*. Princeton: Princeton University Press.

Singer, J. D. 1987. Reconstructing the correlates of war dataset on material capabilities of states, 1816–1985. *International Interactions*, **14**(2), 115–132.

Smith, T. 2000. *Foreign Attachments: The Power of Ethnic Groups in the Making of American Foreign Policy*. Cambridge: Harvard University Press.

Snyder, J. 1991. *Myths of Empire: Domestic Politics and International Ambition*. Ithaca: Cornell University Press.

Solingen, E. 1998. *Regional Orders at Century's Dawn: Global and Domestic Influences on Grand Strategy*. Princeton: Princeton University Press.

Solingen, E. 2007. *Nuclear Logics: Contrasting Paths in East Asia and the Middle East*. Princeton: Princeton University Press.

Staton, J. K. and Moore, W. H. 2011. Judicial power in domestic and international politics. *International Organization*, **65**(3), 553–587.

Sudduth, J. K. 2017. Strategic logic of elite purges in dictatorships. *Comparative Political Studies*, **50**(13), 1768–1801.

Svolik, M. W. 2012. *The Politics of Authoritarian Rule*. Cambridge: Cambridge University Press.

Thacker, S. C. 1999. The high politics of IMF lending. *World Politics*, **52**(1), 38–75.

Tingley, D. 2010. Donors and domestic politics: Political influences on foreign aid effort. *The Quarterly Review of Economics and Finance*, **50**(1), 40–49.

Trubowitz, P. 1998. *Defining the National Interest: Conflict and Change in American Foreign Policy*. Chicago: University of Chicago Press.

Tsebelis, G., 2002. *Veto Players: How Political Institutions Work*. Princeton: Princeton University Press.

Vengroff, R. 1976. Instability and foreign policy behavior: Black Africa in the UN. *American Journal of Political Science*, **20**(3), 425–438.

Verdier, P. H. and Versteeg, M. 2019. Separation of powers, treaty-making, and treaty withdrawal in C. A. Bradley (ed.), *The Oxford Handbook of Comparative Foreign Relations Law*. New York: Oxford University Press. https://global.oup.com/academic/product/the-oxford-handbook-of-compara tive-foreign-relations-law-9780190653330?cc=us&lang=en&#

Voeten, E. 2000. Clashes in the assembly. *International Organization*, **54**(2), 185–215.

Waldner, D. and Lust, E. 2018. Unwelcome change: Coming to terms with democratic backsliding. *Annual Review of Political Science*, **21**, 93–113.

Walt, S. M. 1987. *The Origins of Alliance*. Ithaca: Cornell University Press.

Weeks, J. L. 2014. *Dictators at War and Peace*. Ithaca: Cornell University Press.

Wiegandt, M. H. 1995. Germany's international integration: The rulings of the German federal constitutional court on the Maastricht Treaty and the out-of-area deployment of German troops. *American University International Law Review*, **10**(2), 889–916.

Wilson, M. C. and Woldense, J. 2019. Contested or established? A comparison of legislative powers across regimes. *Democratization*, **26**(4), 585–605.

Yarhi-Milo, K. 2018. *Who Fights for Reputation: The Psychology of Leaders in International Conflict*. Princeton: Princeton University Press.

Yarhi-Milo, K., Kertzer, J. D. and Renshon, J. 2018. Tying hands, sinking costs, and leader attributes. *Journal of Conflict Resolution*, **62**(10), 2150–2179.

Acknowledgments

This research was supported by the US National Science Foundation (SES-0921830). We are very grateful to Jesse Johnson, Naoko Matsumura, Alex Pugh, and Eelco van der Maat for their leading roles as research assistants on the CHISOLS dataset, and to Kristin Bryant, Nicholas Coulombe, and Alex Pugh for research assistance on this study. We benefited significantly from opportunities to present this research to many audiences. We are thankful for insights from discussants and audience members at meetings of the American Political Science Association, the International Studies Association, and the Agreements, Law, and International Politics workshop at Rice University, as well as seminars at Texas A&M University, Texas Christian University, the University of California Santa Barbara, the University of Colorado, the University of Notre Dame, the University of Texas-Dallas, and the University of Wisconsin–Madison. Finally, we feel fortunate to have received valuable feedback from our colleagues at Rice University and University of California, Berkeley. This Element is dedicated to our children, Gavin and Julia Woods and Oliver Mattes-Yamamoto.

Cambridge Elements $\overline{\overline{}}$

International Relations

Series Editors

Jon C. W. Pevehouse
University of Wisconsin–Madison

Jon C. W. Pevehouse is the Vilas Distinguished Achievement Professor of Political Science at the University of Wisconsin–Madison. He has published numerous books and articles in IR in the fields of international political economy, international organizations, foreign policy analysis, and political methodology. He is a former editor of the leading IR field journal, International Organization.

Tanja A. Börzel
Freie Universität Berlin

Tanja A. Börzel is the Professor of political science and holds the Chair for European Integration at the Otto-Suhr-Institute for Political Science, Freie Universität Berlin. She holds a PhD from the European University Institute, Florence, Italy. She is coordinator of the Research College "The Transformative Power of Europe," as well as the FP7-Collaborative Project "Maximizing the Enlargement Capacity of the European Union" and the H2020 Collaborative Project "The EU and Eastern Partnership Countries: An Inside-Out Analysis and Strategic Assessment." She directs the Jean Monnet Center of Excellence "Europe and its Citizens."

Edward D. Mansfield
University of Pennsylvania

Edward D. Mansfield is the Hum Rosen Professor of Political Science, University of Pennsylvania. He has published well over 100 books and articles in the area of international political economy, international security, and international organizations. He is Director of the Christopher H. Browne Center for International Politics at the University of Pennsylvania and former program co-chair of the American Political Science Association.

Editorial Team

International Relations Theory
Jeffrey T. Checkel, European University Institute, Florence
Miles Kahler, American University Washington, D.C.

International Security
Sarah Kreps, Cornell University
Anna Leander, Graduate Institute Geneva

International Political Economy
Edward D. Mansfield, University of Pennsylvania
Stafanie Walter, University of Zurich

International Organisations
Tanja A. Börzel, Freie Universität Berlin
Jon C. W. Pevehouse, University of Wisconsin–Madison

Cambridge Elements ≡

International Relations

Elements in the series

Printed in the United States
by Baker & Taylor Publisher Services